FOR THE LOVE OF DEATH

SRISHTI BHARDWAJ

BookLeaf Publishing
India | USA | UK

Presentation by *BookLeaf Publishing*

Web: www.bookleafpub.com
E-mail: info@bookleafpub.com

ISBN: 9789369540433

First edition 2025

ACKNOWLEDGEMENT

First and foremost, I extend my deepest gratitude to the Almighty for His endless blessings, guidance, and inspiration throughout this journey. Without His grace, this novel would have remained a distant dream.

I owe my heartfelt thanks to my parents whose unwavering love, support, and encouragement have been my greatest source of strength. Their belief in me has always been the wind beneath my wings.

To my brother, thank you for being my pillar of support and my constant cheerleader. Your faith in me and my work has meant more than words can express.

This novel is as much yours as it is mine, for without each of you, this would not have been possible.

PROLOGUE

They say death arrives without warning, an unseen shadow slipping into your life and altering it forever. I used to think it was just something people said to sound wise—a dramatic statement about life's unpredictability. But now, I know better. Death is real, and it doesn't knock before entering. It doesn't ask for permission to rearrange your world. And sometimes, it looks at you with stormy gray eyes.

It all started the day Seema Ma'am confiscated my novel and hurled it to the ground like it was cursed. I didn't think much of it at the time—just another embarrassing episode in the circus that was my school life. I couldn't have known how quickly things would spiral after that. The night we visited the cemetery, on a dare that seemed stupid even then, everything changed. That's when I met him.

I still remember the way the rain blurred my vision and the cold seeped into my bones as I knelt beside him. His wounds were deep, blood pooling around him like an accusation, yet his face was calm, almost serene. I wanted to run, but something about him held me there.

Maybe it was the way he looked at me—not with fear or desperation, but with a strange, quiet recognition.

"You shouldn't be here," he had whispered, his voice as fragile as the storm raging around us. "Leave while you still can."

But I didn't leave. Instead, I stayed and tied a handkerchief around his bleeding leg, as if that tiny gesture could somehow mend whatever was broken in him. That was the night I first saw the shadows that followed him, the ones that seemed to stretch further than the rain-soaked ground. And that was the night he entered my life, as uninvited as the storm that brought him.

Reyansh—that's what I chose to call him. Back then, he was just a mystery, a fleeting encounter that should have faded into memory but didn't. He lingered—in my thoughts, in my dreams, and eventually, in my reality. He's not like anyone I've ever met. He's not like anyone, period.

It took me a while to understand what he was, to piece together the fragments of truth he reluctantly shared. Reyansh isn't human. He told me I shouldn't get involved, that his world would only bring me pain. But how could I not? He saved me when no one else could—not just from danger, but from myself.

Now, as I sit in my parents' empty house, their laughter is replaced by a silence so loud it hurts, I feel his presence.

He's always near, watching, waiting. My friends think I'm crazy for trusting him, for letting him into my life. Maybe I am. But there's something about Reyansh that feels inevitable, like a thread of fate I can't unravel.

I've asked him why he stays. "Because our story isn't over," he says. But what does that even mean? Am I some unfinished business, a task he has to complete before he moves on? Or is there something deeper, something neither of us fully understands?

As the clock ticks past midnight, I realize I'm not afraid anymore. Whatever lies ahead—whether answers or more questions, salvation or destruction—I'm ready. Because loving death means embracing the unknown, and with Reyansh by my side, I'm willing to risk everything.

I

I had just stepped back into the hallway after filling my water bottle when I saw all the girls spilling out of the classroom, gathering in clumps. The air was thick with tension, and whispers floated around like restless spirits. Pushing through the crowd, I spotted my girl gang huddled in a corner, their heads bent together in urgent conversation.

"Hey! I just went to fill my water bottle and I guess I missed some drama. What's going on?" I asked, a bit breathless, my heart pounding with a mix of curiosity and dread.

"As usual, Seema Ma'am ordered the monitors to go through our belongings. Someone said we're hiding novels in our bags," Meera replied, glaring at Avantika, our class monitor with a look of pure disgust that could melt steel.

My heart sank as I suddenly remembered the novel I'd bought this morning at the school book fair. "Guys, I have a novel in my bag."

They all stared at me, eyes wide with shock.

"You're done for today. Hitler isn't going to let you off easy," Meera said, shaking her head, her voice a low whisper of doom.

"Don't worry, you're not alone. My lipstick is in the bag. She'll call me out too," Anaya added, rolling her eyes with a mix of defiance and resignation.

We all watched intently as Avantika rummaged through the bags, pulling out any "forbidden items" and handing them over to Seema Ma'am, or as we liked to call her, Hitler Ma'am. The classroom, usually a place of mundane boredom, had turned into a scene of high drama. When she reached my seat and pulled out my precious, newly bought green-covered novel, her expression shifted from serious to a sinister smile. She walked over to our teacher and handed my novel to her. Seema Ma'am's face twisted with anger as she looked at me, then she threw the novel onto the floor with a thud.

Finally, the chaos settled, and we were called back into the classroom. The room buzzed with murmurs, which immediately ceased when Seema Ma'am slammed the duster on the desk, sending a cloud of chalk dust into the air.

"What is there to talk about?" Seema Ma'am snapped, her voice sharp. "You young girls have no decency. How many times have I told you not to read novels? These novels are just meant to brainwash you. Instead, read books that would enhance your knowledge. Despite my many reminders, you girls don't listen. Today, all those caught will have a meeting with the principal, and their parents will be called," she began calling out names one by one, scolding the girls not only for owning novels, but for other things too like magazines, make-up, etc. Finally, she called my name.

"Sia, your grades have already fallen because of these mindless novels. Do you even want a good future for yourself? Why is your name in every mischievous activity? Now I will return this novel to your parents only."

I mumbled an apology and sat down, my cheeks burning with shame and anger.

We were scolded by the principal, and our parent-teacher meeting got scheduled in the coming week. This was becoming a regular occurrence for us. Seema Ma'am was so particular about these things. She always said that 16-year-old girls like us were common prey for predators as we are immature and dreamy. According to her, we should protect ourselves by focusing only on study and nothing else. After returning from the principal's office, I slumped into my seat and yawned. Anaya, who had also been scolded for her favorite lipstick, sat behind me. She started talking about how she had bought it with her pocket money and how her mother knew nothing about it, cursing Avantika a few times in frustration.

"I acknowledge that we had a heavy day today, but our plan is still on, friends. No one is backing out," Meera whispered, her eyes gleaming with determination.

"Do you see the weather today? Do you really think it's a good day for this? It's going to rain heavily. Believe me," I tried to reason with her, glancing at the darkening skies outside.

"Exactly, Sia. This is the perfect time to visit the cemetery and interact with ghosts. Did you forget about the ghost sightings in some students' photographs taken at the cemetery? Spooky weather makes it more interesting," Meera explained, her excitement palpable.

"I agree with Meera. I need content for my social media channel. It's been so long since I posted something... and I have a better idea," Anaya said with a mischievous smile that promised trouble.

"Let's take Avantika with us. Let her cry and scream in fear while we record her," she laughed devilishly and looked at us for confirmation.

I shook my head. "Why would you do that to her? Let her live in peace. No need to involve others."

"As if she cares about us. Don't you know who's responsible for today's incident? She was the one who told Hitler about the novels. This is our chance for revenge," Anaya huffed, her voice tinged with anger.

"Let's take her too. It'll be fun," Meera said, brushing off my concerns with a wave of her hand.

"Hey Avantika... come here for a moment. We have something to ask you," Anaya called out.

Avantika looked at us and rolled her eyes but still came over, curiosity getting the better of her.

"We're planning to visit the cemetery near our school, but we're afraid to go alone. Would you like to join us? If there's one brave person with us, we won't be scared," Anaya said sweetly, her voice dripping with false sincerity.

"I'd rather join a gang of dacoits than follow you guys on your stupid adventures," she huffed and rolled her eyes.

"We respect your opinion, Avantika. It's perfectly fine if you don't want to join," I said, but Meera and Anaya shot me a look that clearly conveyed I was jeopardizing their plans.

"Come on, Avantika. It'll be so much fun. You'll enjoy it, I promise," Meera interjected, her tone coaxing and persuasive.

Avantika looked at us suspiciously but eventually said yes.

I knew we'd be in big trouble if Avantika didn't enjoy the trip, as the news would no doubt reach Hitler's ears, but who could explain that to my mischievous friends?

II

"Mumma! I'm going out to meet Anaya and Meera," I shouted as I hastily shoved my feet into my shoes.

"It's pouring outside. What's so important that you need to go out in this weather?" my mother grumbled, emerging from the kitchen to hand me an umbrella.

"I told you, it's for a group assignment due tomorrow. Otherwise, why would I go out at this time?" I tried to act cute and convincing, but my mother just shook her head in resignation and walked back to the kitchen.

"Just be back in time for dinner," she called out as I closed the front door behind me.

The weather outside was dangerously alluring, with dark clouds blanketing the sky and raindrops pelting the ground as if waging war. The lush greenery of Shimla, nestled in the Himalayas, looked both beautiful and foreboding under the stormy skies. Even with an umbrella, I couldn't stay completely dry and was half-drenched by the time I reached our meeting point, a rain shelter near the cemetery. Twilight had already settled in, and darkness was beginning to envelop us. Anaya was already there, her tall, slim figure with dusky, beautiful skin and curly hair easily recognizable even in the dim light.

"I'm so sorry, guys. The weather made me late," I said as I stepped into the shelter.

"It's okay. Our chief guest is also late," Anaya said, hinting at Avantika.

"Do you really think she'll come? After all, we aren't exactly on good terms," I reasoned.

"Don't worry. Look behind you," Anaya replied.

I turned to see Avantika, her tall figure enveloped in a beautiful pink raincoat. Her fair skin glistened like rose petals under the water droplets on her face, and her long, flowing hair was tucked neatly under the raincoat's hood.

"I shouldn't have agreed to your plans," she grumbled as she joined us under the shelter.

"But now you have," Meera replied cheerfully. "So, are you all ready for some adventure?" she asked, her short stature and shoulder-length hair framing her face, her specs glinting with excitement.

We all shouted "yes" together, but Avantika just mumbled a reluctant assent.

Meera pulled out a small Ouija board from her bag and began laying out the rules. "Before we enter the cemetery, remember a few rules," she said, her tone suddenly serious.

"We're here to meet the souls of the cemetery, not to disturb them. We must respect their privacy and not disrespect them in any way. Also, whatever happens, everyone must follow my rules. Nobody leaves or runs away without my approval, or the spirits will follow you wherever you go."

The intensity in her voice made us shiver, but we decided to follow her lead since she was into these spooky things. Meanwhile, Anaya took out her phone and started her vlog.

The roads to the cemetery were deserted, and the trees lining either side created an eerie atmosphere. As we approached the gates, Meera stopped us.

"Guys, beware of the grumpy old man who lives near the cemetery. I've heard he guards the place and doesn't let anyone in except the families of the deceased."

Meera led us cautiously towards the large iron gate of the cemetery. There was no one guarding it. It struck us as odd – there was a big gate but no boundary wall, so anyone could have entered from any side. The entire cemetery was surrounded by jungle.

Meera reminded us of the rules again before opening the gates. Anaya clung to Meera, holding her hand, while Avantika stuck close to me, shivering with either cold or fear.

We followed Meera in silence as she lit the dark path with a torch. We had no idea what was happening ahead because of the heavy rain, and we were entirely relying on Meera to guide us when suddenly, she screamed and bolted back to the gates. The whole place echoed with our shouts as we ran after her for safety. In the chaos, Avantika accidentally pushed me, and I fell, bruising my elbow and knees.

When I got up, I saw that they were already gone. I tried to run, but then I heard a low growl. I wanted to keep running, but the growl sounded like someone was hurt.

Though I was still trembling with fear, I turned around to see the source of our terror. The torch Meera had dropped in her panic was still on, its light revealing a figure in a dire state. His clothes were tattered, and his legs had deep, bleeding wounds. Despite his condition, his features were striking — almost ethereal in their perfection, with chiseled cheekbones, a strong jawline, and full, sensuous lips. His eyes, a captivating shade of deep, enigmatic gray, were framed by thick, dark lashes that seemed to hold a world of secrets. They glinted with a curious mix of youthful energy and ancient wisdom. His hair was a cascade of jet-black waves, falling just above his shoulders, framing his face with a natural, effortless elegance. He seemed to be in his early twenties.

There was something enchanting yet haunting about his presence. I hesitated, but then took a step towards him, noticing how severe his wounds were as blood poured from them. Panic surged through me, and I didn't know what to do. Quickly, I pulled out my handkerchief and tied it around his severely wounded leg. The small piece of cloth barely helped in controlling the bleeding.

"Please wait here while I call an ambulance," I said, reaching for my phone. But he suddenly clutched my hand, making me jump in fear.

"Please don't... I will be fine," he said, his breath ragged.

"Let me call my parents then. Otherwise, how will I help you?" I pleaded, but he still shook his head.

I removed the shirt I was wearing over my top and started cleaning his wounds. My actions were involuntary, driven by sheer instinct, and nothing seemed under my control. As I focused on his wounds, I felt his gaze on me, but I ignored it, concentrating on cleaning the injuries. Then, I heard the frantic shouts of my friends calling my name from the other side of the gate.

I looked into his eyes, a small smile of hope forming on my lips. "Wait here while I bring them inside. We'll treat your wounds."

I ran to the gate and was engulfed in a hug by all three of them. "Thank God you're safe," Anaya said, tears in her eyes.

"To hell with this game, let's go back. It's already late," Meera said.

"No, wait. There's a wounded boy inside." They looked at me with confused expressions but agreed to follow.

I led them back to where I had left him, but when we arrived, there was no one there. Only the torch flickered, casting light on an empty space.

III

"These young girls think they can get away with any mischief without consequences. The four of you are suspended for a week. Bring your parents to the next parent-teacher meeting," the principal said with utter disappointment, adjusting her horn-rimmed spectacles on her nose.

Our adventure to the cemetery spread through the school like wildfire, accompanied by various rumors: I was attacked by a ghost, or I fought off a spirit that wanted to turn me into sand. Everyone seemed to enjoy the gossip, except me. In an all-girls school, even the smallest news becomes extraordinary.

"How are we going to tell our parents about our suspension? Mine don't even know I went to the cemetery," I huffed, slouching in my seat.

"Mine have no idea either," Anaya said, sitting beside me.

"Let's not tell our parents. We can leave home in our school uniforms and go somewhere else," Meera suggested, earning glares from Anaya and me.

"Sooner or later, we have to tell our parents. We can't hide it; they'll find out at the parent-teacher meeting anyway. What's the point of hiding it? We'll just get into more trouble," I said, and Anaya sighed.

Meanwhile, Avantika was crying on the front bench as if someone had died. Her group of friends consoled her while she loudly cursed us.

"Don't dump your fault on us. You were the one who agreed to go with us. We didn't force or kidnap you," Meera snapped, fed up with Avantika's endless ranting.

With great difficulty, we managed to get Meera out of the class to avoid another bout of trouble for fighting with the class monitor.

"Let it go, Meer—" I began, but my eyes caught sight of a familiar figure—the same man I had met in the cemetery. He looked fully healed, with no trace of the severe wounds from the day before. Dressed in a long black coat and trousers, with his hair neatly tucked under a hat, he appeared even more handsome.

He was so mesmerizing that I forgot all my worries just looking at him. Hypnotized again, I started walking towards him, ignoring the confused glances from my friends. I didn't want to waste time explaining.

As I approached, his lips twitched into a smile. He was standing on the other side of the gate. I asked the guard to let me out for a few minutes, claiming the person outside was my relative. After much insistence, he reluctantly agreed, and I stepped out to see his beautiful smile up close.

"What a coincidence! We meet again," I said shyly, tucking a few strands of hair behind my ears and blushing.

"I don't think it's a coincidence," he said in a voice that made my heart flutter. "I came here because I wanted to see you."

He grinned, and I felt my cheeks flush even more, but his words sparked a question in my mind. "How do you know about my school?" I asked curiously.

"Would you believe me if I said I just guessed?" he replied in a raspy voice.

"I... I..." I stammered, unable to form words.

He laughed at my flustered expression. "I wanted to personally thank you for your help the other day and return your shirt. I found your marksheet in the shirt pocket. The paper was mostly destroyed by the rain and when you used it to clean my wounds, but the school logo remained intact."

I suddenly realized that I had hidden it in my shirt's pocket so that my mother couldn't find it. I had again scored very less marks in physics. He handed me the shirt, and as our fingers brushed, something shifted in his expression. His smile disappeared, replaced by a sudden look of dread. I was about to retract my hand when he suddenly grasped it, looking at me with the same intense expression. We stood like that for what felt like an eternity when he finally released my hands.

"Run, save them. Save your parents. You have to save them," he said urgently, as if warning me.

Then, just like that, he vanished into thin air, leaving me utterly perplexed. I returned to the gate and pleaded with the guard to let me use his phone for an urgent call. He reluctantly handed it over. I dialed my mother's number, but no one answered. Then, I tried my father's number, but it was switched off. Panic started to set in. By now, Meera and Anaya had also reached the main gate.

I ran towards them, handing the phone back to the guard. "Something is terribly wrong. My parents aren't picking up my calls," I said, feeling the onset of an anxiety attack.

They tried to calm me down. Anaya fetched a water bottle from the class while Meera gently made me sit on the stairs near the gate. I was breathing heavily, repeating over and over that something was wrong. It took a while for me to calm down, and when I did, I was called to the principal's office.

When I knocked and was given permission to enter, the principal's expression was completely different from when she had scolded us earlier. Seema Ma'am was also there, her usually stern demeanor softened.

I could sense that something wasn't right. They hesitated, wanting to say something, but were cautious with their words. Finally, with a deep sigh, the principal began, "I know what I am about to say will be hard on you, but my child, God is with you."

I didn't understand what she was trying to say, but I had a sinking feeling. I didn't want to hear her next words.

Seema Ma'am spoke next, her voice filled with compassion. "Your parents were on their way somewhere in their car when they met with an accident. They are admitted to the hospital."

It felt like a thunderbolt had struck me. Suddenly, everything around me started to blur— the table, the cupboards, the principal, even Seema Ma'am. Everything turned dark, and the last thing I heard was a loud thud.

IV

My world had turned upside down in these three months. Everything changed with my parents' death, a tragedy that I wasn't ready to face. I never dreamed of a situation like this. I had no idea how to deal with it. But here I was, somehow surviving through the days—barely living. After my parents' death, my uncle and aunt wanted to take me with them, but I couldn't muster up the courage to leave my house, which still held the faint fragrance of my parents' memories.

For a month, I was absent from school, busy with all the rituals and seeing the guests who came to mourn. I still feel that it is a dream and not reality—a dream I wanted to wake up from. I cried and I howled, but nothing changed. I had to live with this reality. The pain of loss will always be there. However, I had somehow become accustomed to it.

After a month, I threw myself into the schoolwork I had missed during this time. It helped me to forget, even if just for a while. But no matter how busy I kept myself, my heart still ached constantly, as if a big thorn had lodged itself deep inside.

I also distanced myself from my friends, becoming unusually quiet, which somehow impressed Seema Ma'am. Despite their best efforts to help me return to my old self, I had no desire to engage. No one can restore you unless you're willing to, and I had no interest in doing so. My only goal was to get through each day without falling apart.

"Don't forget to bring your assignment tomorrow," Jaiveer Sir, our physics teacher, said as he left the classroom. He had the last lecture of the day, and I was grateful for that since last lectures are usually shorter. Physics was the class I dreaded the most.

I packed my bag and left the classroom as usual. I used to go home with Anaya and Meera, but since my parents' death, I spent my days alone. Initially, they used to run after me to catch up, but now they had left me to myself. I didn't feel like spending time with anyone. All I wanted was to drown in my own agony.

As I reached the school gate, I saw a familiar face looking at me. It had been so long since I had seen him. He still looked the same—enchanting and mysterious. The day I met him and he warned me about my parents' mishap replayed in my head. I slowly walked toward him. He looked at me with a sad smile and handed me a bouquet of white orchids with a red rose in the middle.

I took it and thanked him. "You already knew about them. Did you prepare the bouquet the same day you told me to save them?" I asked with a hysterical laugh.

He just smiled and patted my head. "You'll be fine soon."

Hearing this from him, all the pain inside my heart resurfaced. I suddenly hugged him, crying like a small child. He simply patted my head, saying everything would turn out for the better.

After what felt like ages, I pulled away and noticed a big wet patch on his coat from my tears. He bent down to my height and said softly, "Let me walk you home."

The walk to my home was spent in silence. As we reached my front gate, I turned to say goodbye when I noticed a red patch on his arm.

"Another wound," I gasped.

"I guess I am a little clumsy, but I am fine," he said, trying to reassure me, but I wasn't convinced.

"Let me clean it," I insisted.

He was about to refuse when I cut him off firmly. "And I insist."

With a reluctant nod, he agreed and followed me.

I took my keys from my bag, unlocked the door, and gestured for him to enter the house.

"Beware, I am not a good guy. It is not wise to let me enter your home. I don't wish to hurt you, but I've only brought you bad luck so far. You shouldn't let me enter…"

Before he could continue, I placed my index finger on his unusually cold lips. It was then I realized he had always been so cold whenever I touched him, whether when he held my hand or when we were at the cemetery.

"How much worse can it get? My parents are dead, and I feel dead inside. What harm can you do? Just come inside. You're the only one who has stirred my soul," I said, looking into his charcoal grey eyes that seemed to draw me in further.

He removed my fingers from his lips slowly and took my hand as he stepped inside. I led him to the living room, which was cozy with soft lighting, a plush couch, and warm-colored walls. A small wooden coffee table stood in the center, surrounded by bookshelves filled with my parents' favorite novels. A large window overlooked the garden, letting in the last rays of the setting sun.

As we walked through the room, I couldn't help but ask, "What's the significance of the red rose among the white orchids?"

He paused, a thoughtful expression crossing his face. "Though the situation has drained the colors from your life, this red rose will always remind you of the vibrant spirit you are. Even in the midst of sorrow, there's a spark of life and hope within you."

His words touched me deeply, adding a layer of meaning to the bouquet I hadn't considered.

I made him sit on the couch and went to the table drawer on the left side of the room to find the first aid kit. His presence made me inexplicably nervous. After rummaging through the drawer, I finally found the first aid box and returned to sit beside him on the couch. I asked him to remove his coat. Underneath, he wore a white shirt that made him look even more handsome, despite the bloodstains. I asked him to take off his shirt too, which he reluctantly did. There was an unusual tension in the air as we sat together. His skin was a pale shade I had never seen before.

Focusing on the wound, I poured antiseptic onto a cotton pad and gently applied it to the cut. He winced, and I blew softly on the wound to ease the sting. As I treated the injury, I felt his eyes on me. After securely bandaging the wound, I looked up at him with a triumphant smile, but the intensity in his gaze hypnotized me. I looked away, but he slowly placed his index finger under my chin, turning my face back to his. His eyes held a mix of emotions—tenderness and care.

"Why?" he whispered.

"Why what?" I replied.

He sighed. "Why are you so nice to me? I am just a stranger. A no one in your life."

"Then be someone of my life," I answered.

"I am just a bad omen. Someone who will destroy you," he said, looking deeply into my eyes, searching for my thoughts.

I broke eye contact and began fidgeting with the first aid box. I didn't want to say anything. I was afraid, but I preferred to remain in oblivion. I didn't want to worry about the possible mishaps he might bring in my life. His presence was enough for me. I didn't want to know anything about him. He was the only one who could wake up my soul.

He gently placed his hand on my cheek, his ice-cold touch somehow warming my skin. "One day, when you discover the truth, you will hate me. But until then, let me cherish your presence in my life. Let me be the reason you find your lost smile. Let me help you regain the strength to confront your fears." With that, he removed his hand, and I instantly missed its warmth.

He put his coat back on, but before leaving, he promised, "I will return again." Then he turned and walked out, leaving me with an overwhelming sense of anticipation and longing.

V

"So, you're saying you fell in love with a guy you've only met a few times, and who is at least two or three years older than you?" Meera's voice dripped with skepticism.

He had brought me back to life. I had decided to renew my lease on living. The pain of my parents' loss would always linger, but I had accepted my fate. He had become my strength, a magnetic force I couldn't resist. He returned my lost vigor. When I was alone in the world, he stood by me and helped me reclaim my life, accompanying me home almost every day. I started taking baby steps back into the world and eventually reconnected with my friends. They were elated when I first approached them. "I never said I love him. I just admire him. There's something mysterious and attractive about him," I reasoned with Meera.

"The way you talk about him makes him sound like more than just an acquaintance. He's clearly special to you. What's his name?" Anaya asked.

I suddenly realized I didn't know his name, even though it had been a few months since our first meeting in the cemetery.

"I don't know. I never asked," I said. They looked at me as if I had lost my mind.

Anaya took a deep breath, put her hand over her heart, and whispered something to calm herself down.

"Fine, so you don't know his name. Do you have his phone number? His social media account? Anything to contact him?" she asked, crossing her fingers in doubt.

"I have none. I never needed any of that. He's always been there whenever I thought of him," I said, though I felt foolish saying it out loud.

"I hope you at least know where he lives," Meera said with genuine hopelessness, and I reluctantly shook my head.

They looked at me with wide eyes, as if I was speaking an alien language, and they weren't entirely wrong.

I took a deep breath and tried to defend myself. "See, that's what I'm trying to tell you. There is a special connection between us. I never felt the need to know his name, his contact details, or his whereabouts. I feel complete with him, and that's all. I can feel his presence even when he's not with me."

"Anaya, you remember my grandma who can easily tell our past, present, and future just by looking at us," Meera said, and Anaya nodded.

"Luckily, she's visiting us for a few days. Let's meet her. Only she can deal with Sia's weird case. It's out of my hands," Meera said, and Anaya agreed.

I wanted to reason with them, but I decided not to because no matter what I said, they wouldn't be able to understand my feelings. I agreed to meet Meera's grandma, not just to placate my friends, but because it had been a long time since I had seen her. She is such a sweetheart. We used to play with her a lot when we were kids. She used to live with Meera's family, but later, she returned to her village in the mountains. The constant city noise of Shimla didn't suit her; she missed her quiet village life. However, she still visited Meera's family once every few years. She might be in her late eighties now, but she is more active than any of us.

After school, we started walking to Meera's house, which was just about 2km away from the school. As we arrived, the inviting aroma of tea greeted us. Meera's home was a charming house, built with stone walls and a sloping wooden roof, adorned with colorful flower pots on the windowsills. Her mother warmly welcomed us, her smile as bright as the flowers outside.

We went straight to meet Grandma. She was sitting on a warm mat on the floor, shelling peanuts while watching some daily soap opera. She wore traditional pahadi attire—a vibrant, embroidered dress with a woolen shawl draped over her shoulders, her silver hair neatly tied back hidden in her dhattu, and her face lined with the gentle marks of age and wisdom. Her eyes twinkled with the same warmth I remembered from childhood.

As we greeted her, she gave us her blessings and expressed her condolences for my parents. We talked about our school lives while having tea and peanuts. Slowly, the conversation shifted towards me. Though my friends didn't tell her about the mysterious guy, they mentioned that I was having strange experiences lately.

Grandma told me to come and sit beside her. She held my hand and closed her eyes, her face becoming serious. When she opened her eyes, they were filled with a storm of emotions.

"Death is lingering here," she said, and everyone gasped.

Her words hung in the air, heavy and unsettling. I felt a chill run down my spine. I didn't want to hear more about death; it had been my companion for far too long.

"Grandma, what do you mean?" Meera asked, her voice trembling.

Grandma looked at me with a mixture of concern and curiosity. "There is a presence around you, my child. Someone who does not belong to this world, yet lingers close to you."

I shivered at her words, the weight of her gaze making me feel exposed. My mind raced back to the guy who had warned me about my parents and had been a silent support ever since.

"Do you know who it is?" Anaya asked, her voice barely above a whisper.

"His aura is strong. He is connected to death, yet he brings you comfort," Grandma said, her eyes never leaving mine.

I felt a lump in my throat. "Grandma, he… he's the only one who makes me feel alive again…. and he is a human. Believe me," I confessed, tears welling up in my eyes.

Grandma's expression softened. "Sometimes, the ones who seem the most unlikely can become our greatest support. But be careful, child. From what I can sense, his world is not our world, and the connection you share with him may bring havoc in your or his life."

Her words resonated deeply within me. I knew she was right. My mysterious friend had brought me back to life, but there was so much I didn't know about him. I had to be careful, but I also couldn't deny the bond we shared.

"Thank you, Grandma," I whispered, feeling a mix of gratitude and fear.

Grandma patted my hand gently. "Remember, Sia, you are stronger than you think. Trust your instincts and stay true to your heart."

As we left Meera's house that evening, my mind was a whirlwind of thoughts and emotions. The path ahead seemed more uncertain than ever.

VI

He was there again, waiting near the school gates. It had been a week since I'd last seen him, and there was so much to share. As usual, I began walking toward him, almost in a trance, when suddenly I felt a firm grip on my wrist. I turned to find Meera's eyes fixed on me, her grip tightening with concern.

"I can't let you go with him. He's dangerous, Sia," she said, her voice trembling with worry.

"We don't even know what he really is. What if he's just luring you in to hurt you? Use your brain, buddy," Anaya added, her tone stern and anxious.

"Guys, I've been with him for about three months now. I know him better than anyone. He will be the last person to harm me. Please, let me go. He's there for me," I pleaded.

They both knew how stubborn I could be. Meera released my wrist reluctantly, but I could see the concern still etched on her face.

I mouthed "I love you" to them before running towards him.

As usual, he greeted me with a warm smile as I reached him, slightly out of breath from running. He took my bag from me, and we began to walk together.

"Where have you been? There's so much to tell you about what's been going on with me," I said, my excitement barely contained.

"Sorry I couldn't be there. I was caught up with work. I hope nothing too serious happened," he said, gently patting my head.

"Don't worry. It's not that big of a deal—just some deathly things," I chuckled, glancing at him.

He tilted his head, his expression inquisitive.

Before I could respond to his questioning gaze, I noticed that we were heading in a different direction from my home.

"Hey! We're going the wrong way," I said, trying to get his attention, but he just smiled.

"I've found a special place for us. I want to take you there," he said, his eyes sparkling with excitement.

As we walked, I realized that we were headed towards the cemetery where we had first met.

"Remember this place?" he asked, a smile gracing his godlike features.

"The place of the dead where I met life," I replied, but his expression grew solemn.

"You give me more credit than I deserve," he said with a sigh.

"Look at yourself through my eyes, and you'll see who you really are," I said, holding his icy cold hand.

To lighten the mood, I joked, "So, this is your new hangout spot?"

He chuckled softly. "No, it's just a few minutes away."

Curiosity piqued, I followed him to this mysterious location. We arrived at a beautiful meadow nestled among the hills, with a small, abandoned barn in the center. He held my hand as he guided me through the broken fence towards the barn. Gently releasing my hand, he opened the door.

Although I didn't expect much from the rundown place, I was pleasantly surprised to find it clean and well-kept inside, with five lanterns hanging in each corner of the room and one in the middle. He had created a makeshift bed from haystacks, covered with a worn but clean sheet. Though the bed was far from comfortable, his presence made it feel special.

"I wanted to create a special place for us. For you and me. I know it's not what you might have imagined, but…" he began to say, but I stopped him with a gentle touch on his hand.

"I love this place. Now I know where to come whenever I miss you," I said with a smile, and he returned it warmly.

He rested his head gently on my shoulder, emitting a contented sigh. In that moment, it felt as though I had everything I could ever desire—there was no longer a need for anything more in my life.

"Where did you drift off to?" he asked after a few minutes of silence.

"Just a few days ago, my friends were curious about your name," I replied, playing with his hair.

"And what did you tell them?" he asked with genuine curiosity.

"The truth... that I never asked you for your name," I answered.

"And what was their reaction?" he inquired.

"They think I've lost my mind. How can I trust someone whose name I don't even know?" I sighed.

"Well, they're not entirely wrong," he said, chuckling softly before settling deeper into my shoulder.

"Do you think so too? If you do, then tell me about yourself," I urged.

"Now you want to know about me? Earlier, you were content just having me around," he replied.

"That's still true. I feel the same way even now. Knowing your name or details doesn't change how I feel about you," I said.

"I don't have a name," he whispered.

I gently pulled away so I could meet his gaze, struggling to believe what I was hearing. How could someone not have a name?

"That can't be true. If you don't want to tell me, that's fine, but don't feed me absurd lies," I said.

"It's true. I don't have a name. No one has ever called me anything. I've never interacted with anyone but you," he said, his words carrying an air of deep sincerity.

"I can't imagine what your life must be like. It's sad that no one has ever called you by a name. May I give you one?" I asked, and he nodded.

After thinking long and hard, I found the perfect name for him.

"Reyansh… I'll call you Reyansh, meaning 'ray of light.' You are my ray of light in this darkness," I said with a smile.

VII

The hum of computer fans filled the room, merging with the clacking of keyboards and the faint buzz of student chatter. I was immersed in my HTML assignment, struggling to make sense of the lines of code, when Megha slid a folded note onto my desk. She glanced over at Meera, who was watching me expectantly, and I sighed. Our computer teacher was preoccupied with another student on the far side of the lab, so I cautiously unfolded the slip of paper, glancing around to make sure I wasn't being watched.

"We found the identity of your mystery man. Come switch seats with Anaya."

I suppressed an eye roll. Meera was still investigating Reyansh, digging into things I'd told them to leave alone. They didn't understand our connection, and I doubted anyone would. Anaya had already vacated her seat beside Meera and, crouching low, she shuffled her way towards me, using the computers as cover. She whispered for me to switch, and I mimicked her stealthy movements, quietly slipping into the empty seat beside Meera.

"Look here, your so-called 'angel of death.' The one who brings death with him is a Grim Reaper. You're spending time with a Grim Reaper," Meera hissed, her voice a mix of fear and exasperation as she pointed at the screen showing an image of a mysterious, cloaked figure.

I stared at her, unperturbed. "I don't care what he is. For me, he's just someone I want to spend time with." I tried to sound confident, but the thought of him being a Grim Reaper had also thrown me for a loop. Still, even if he were a monster, I knew deep down that I wouldn't abandon him.

"You've really gone mad," Meera muttered, shaking her head in disbelief. Before I could respond, Avantika, sitting in the row behind us, shot her hand up.

"Ma'am, I'm unable to focus because Sia and Meera are constantly whispering. They're not even working on HTML—they're just messing around on the internet."

Our teacher's glare could have melted ice. A moment later, Meera and I were ushered out of the lab with a scolding that echoed down the hallway.

"Tell your Grim Reaper to take her with him," Meera grumbled as we walked, her words laced with frustration.

"Why are you trying so hard to make him out as a monster? You don't even know who he is. Why so much judgment?" I asked, the sadness seeping into my voice.

Meera opened her mouth to respond, but the bell rang, cutting her off. Students flooded the corridor, and Avantika passed by, shooting us a smug look.

"Serves you both right," she sneered before disappearing into the throng of classmates.

Anaya joined us moments later, shaking her head. "You guys can't go five minutes without getting caught, can you?"

"I'm just so done with her. How much more do I have to do to get through to her?" Meera said, her frustration bubbling over.

"Still obsessing over him, huh?" Anaya sighed, looking at me with a mix of concern and resignation.

I could feel the tension still lingering. "Let's drop it, okay? Instead of dwelling on all these things that aren't even real, let's head to the canteen. I didn't bring lunch today, so I'll grab something there."

They nodded, but I knew the discussion was far from over.

I loaded my plate with rice, dal, and salad, and made my way to the table where my two personal investigators, Meera and Anaya, were waiting for me. They sat silently as I ate, but their eyes held the conversation they were dying to continue. I took my time, savoring each bite, trying to delay the inevitable. Just as I finished the last spoonful of rice and dal, Meera placed a piece of sweet on my empty plate, her smile gentle but purposeful.

“I know you like these. I brought them specifically for you,” she said, setting a small box of sweets on the table. I raised an eyebrow at her, suspecting there was more to her kindness.

“Sia, we’re not your enemies. We love you. We’re a family,” Meera began, her voice softening as she placed her hand over mine. “I know you don’t want to talk about him with us, but we’re just worried. We don’t want to see you get hurt.”

I sighed, placing my hand on hers. “I know you both care about me, and I appreciate it more than you realize. You’re my only family now. I stayed here even when my relatives wanted me to move away because I couldn’t bear the thought of leaving you two behind. But you need to understand—he’s important to me too. I don’t want to lose him.”

Meera looked at me with a mixture of sympathy and frustration. “So, you’re okay with the fact that he’s a Grim Reaper, roaming around carrying souls with him?”

I took a deep breath, bracing myself against the harsh truth. “It’s not easy to accept, I get that. But he’s not a monster, Meera. He doesn’t kill people—he just guides souls to the afterlife. He’s a bridge, not the cause of their death.”

A heavy silence fell over us, and for a moment, I felt like I'd won this battle. But then Anaya spoke, her words slicing through my fragile sense of victory.

"So, you're okay with the possibility that he might have been the one who took your parents from you?"

Her question hit me like a punch to the gut. I didn't want to consider the possibility. The idea that Reyansh, the person who had brought light back into my life, could also be the reason my parents were gone, was too much to bear.

"Why would he do that?" I whispered, my voice trembling as I struggled to process the thought. "I saved him when he was injured. He wouldn't do something like that."

Anaya leaned forward, her expression unrelenting. "Maybe that's why he's taking care of you now—out of guilt or pity, because you helped him when he needed it. Maybe he's just repaying a debt."

Her words were a thunderbolt, tearing through the thin veil of hope I'd wrapped around myself. My heart felt like it was shattering into a million pieces. Could it be true? Could the one person who had pulled me back from the edge also be the one who had pushed me there in the first place?

***

The sound of raindrops tapping on the windowsill drowned out the teacher's voice, but Anaya's words echoed relentlessly in my mind, each one a sharp sting. I knew the only way to dull this pain was to confront him. As soon as the final bell rang, I sprang from my seat, packed my bag in a flurry, and rushed toward the school gate. I could hear Meera and Anaya calling my name, their footsteps quickening behind me, but I wasn't going to stop until I got the answers I needed.

I burst through the gate, my eyes frantically scanning the street for any sign of him. But he wasn't there today. My heart sank, but I refused to give up. I pivoted and sprinted toward the barn, the rain soaking my clothes and mingling with the storm inside me. My thoughts were tangled in a web of fear and desperation; I wasn't sure if I wanted to find him or run in the opposite direction. I dreaded his answers as much as I needed them.

Reaching the barn, I paused, gasping for breath. There he was, lying in the dim light, his figure hunched and covered in fresh wounds. The sight of him, battered and bleeding, made my heart lurch. For a moment, all my questions faded, replaced by sheer concern. I ran to him, dropping my bag and reaching out instinctively.

"For God's sake, how can you be injured again and again? Are you a gangster or a Grim Reaper?" The words tumbled out before I could stop them, my voice a mix of exasperation and worry.

He looked up sharply, his eyes locking onto mine, a storm of emotions swirling within them. It was the first time I had called him that—to his face. The title hung in the air, heavy and unspoken for so long. My breath caught as the weight of my words hit me. I quickly averted my gaze, fumbling to pull out a water bottle and a handkerchief from my bag to tend to his wounds. I busied myself with cleaning his cuts, trying to ignore the charged silence between us.

He watched me closely, his expression unreadable. He didn't say a word, but his eyes were filled with a thousand questions. I could feel the intensity of his gaze, probing and searching, but I couldn't bring myself to meet it. My hands shook slightly as I dabbed at his wounds, the rain dripping from my hair onto his skin. Every touch felt like a fragile truce between us, one that could shatter at any moment with the wrong question, the wrong answer.

After bandaging his wounds, I stood up, ready to put some distance between us, but he grabbed my arm and pulled me close. His eyes bore into mine, searching for answers to questions he hadn't voiced. His breath was warm against my ear, and the space between us seemed to shrink until it was nonexistent.

"Say it again," he whispered, his voice a low murmur that sent shivers down my spine.

I wanted to pull away, to escape the pull of his presence, but a stronger part of me craved the comfort of his embrace, the safety I'd found in him, even knowing what he truly was. My heart was a storm of conflicting emotions, and the truth felt like a razor on my tongue.

"The angel of death... the darkness that lingers around me.... It's you," I said, my voice quivering as the words tumbled out. "You're not human. You're a Grim Reaper."

My eyes stung with unshed tears, blurring his face. I half expected him to deny it, to tell me I was mistaken, but he simply held my gaze, unwavering. The truth hung heavy between us, an undeniable presence that changed everything and yet, nothing.

"How does this truth change the course of our relationship?" he whispered, his voice soft but insistent, as though daring me to look beyond the surface of what he was.

VIII

I never imagined my life could twist so drastically after my parent's death. The darkness I felt then had seemed like the worst it could get, but now, standing in the arms of a Grim Reaper—the angel of death itself—my reality felt even more surreal. This was the one who carried souls to the afterlife, the one whose presence meant loss and sorrow for others, yet with him, I found something entirely different. Where others wept, I found comfort. Where others feared, I laughed.

But even the strange solace I found in his arms couldn't suppress the gnawing question that threatened to shatter everything. Now, verything hung in the balance, teetering on the edge of a single question. His earlier words echoed in my mind: *"How does this truth change the course of our relationship?"* I realized that his question depended entirely on mine, the one that burned at the back of my throat, threatening to unravel the fragile bond between us. My next question could decide everything—whether we remained tethered by the strange connection we had found or if we would be torn apart by a truth too heavy to bear.

I pulled back slightly, searching his eyes as if I could find the answer there without having to ask. My heart pounded in my chest, a frantic rhythm of fear and hope tangled together. The truth was on the tip of my tongue, burning like an ember, and I knew that once it was spoken, there would be no going back.

"Did you separate my parents from me?"

The words slipped out, each one heavy and laced with the weight of all my pain and uncertainty. The air between us seemed to freeze, and for a moment, I wished I could take it back, wished I could pretend I didn't need to know. But it was too late. The question hung there, raw and exposed, waiting for an answer that could change everything—or confirm the fears I didn't want to admit.

His silence was a universe of its own, stretching between us, unspoken yet deafening. Every second that passed felt like a thread unraveling, pulling apart the fragile connection we had built. My chest tightened with the weight of the truth I both craved and feared.

"Just say it, Reyansh. For once, say the truth," I begged, my voice barely a whisper over the pounding of my heart.

He clenched his jaw, a pained expression shadowing his face as he finally spoke. "You said I'm a Grim Reaper. The answer lies in the truth of my very essence. I did take your parents, Sia. I guided them to the afterlife. That's my job." His words came through gritted teeth, but there was a crack in his voice, a tremor that betrayed the agony he felt in confessing.

The truth hit me like a wrecking ball, shattering what was left of my heart into irreparable pieces. The air felt too thick, like it was suffocating me, pressing down until I thought I might break under its weight. I wanted to flee from this new reality, to run away from the darkness that threatened to consume me—but I couldn't. Not yet. There was still one more question that burned in my mind, and I couldn't leave without hearing the answer. I needed all the answers today, no matter how much they hurt.

My silence only seemed to make him more anxious. He tried to close the distance between us, but I stepped back, raising my hand. "Don't come near."

His eyes widened, and the distance between us became a chasm I wasn't sure we could ever cross again. "So, you spent all this time with me… Was it all out of pity? Or did you actually care about me?" I crossed my fingers behind my back, dreading the answer. Pity—the one word I never wanted to hear.

"What do you think?" he whispered, his voice wavering.

"I have no clue," I shot back, my voice cracking. "Not after everything I've learned today. I don't know what to expect from you anymore—the one who took away my happiness and then tried to replace it. Was it pity? Or was it something else?" I bit down on the tears that threatened to spill, swallowing the lump in my throat.

Silence again. But this one was louder, more deafening than any of his words had ever been.

"I want to hear it, Reyansh! For god's sake… speak up!" My voice trembled as I raised it, desperate for clarity, for something to make sense.

His shoulders slumped, and his gaze dropped to the ground. "The day before your parents' death, you treated my wounds. No one except you had ever done that. Every time I was hurt, you held me, Sia. You took my hand. How could I not feel indebted to you?" His voice was soft now, broken. "I didn't want to take your parents, but their time had come. I'm part of nature. And nature never bends its rules. At first, I stayed out of pity… I wanted to repay you because I felt I owed you. But as I kept spending time with you—"

"Stop," I cut him off, my voice sharp. I couldn't take it anymore. "You understand each syllable you've just spoken, don't you? I free you from whatever debt you think you owe me. Let's never meet again, Reyansh. Not in this life, not ever. I don't even want to see you at the time of my death." I turned to leave, but his hand shot out, gripping my wrist with a force that made me yelp in pain.

Before I could lash out, I caught his expression—fear. The same terror I'd seen that day when he warned me about my parents. His grip tightened, leaving imprints of his fingers on my skin, and I winced as he finally let go.

"Go away… forever," he said, his lips quivering, but his eyes—his eyes pleaded for something else. They begged me to stay. "You're right… let's not meet again in this life." His voice wavered, raw and fragile.

I stood there, paralyzed by the contradiction between his words and his gaze. Then, his face twisted into something primal, a roar ripping from his throat. "Just go, Sia, before I take you with me… forever."

That was it. I ran. I ran faster than I ever had in my life, bursting out of the barn and into the storm outside. The rain lashed down in sheets, the thunder growling overhead as if the sky itself was warning me to keep running. I bolted through the trees, the dark shapes looming and twisting in the shadows, making everything feel eerie and wrong. The wind howled in my ears, drowning out the sound of my own breath.

I had just crossed the cemetery when I saw it—a car. Its headlights cut through the dark, blinding me as it swerved toward me, horn blaring. I tried to move, but my legs gave way beneath me. My vision blurred, and the world spun as I collapsed onto the road, the roar of the storm fading into silence as everything went black.

When I regained consciousness, I found myself sitting beside a grave, soaked to the bone, with the rain still pouring down in thick sheets. A man in his late thirties was crouched in front of me, holding an umbrella over my head. His face, though rugged, was marked by concern.

"Drink some water," he said gently, offering me a bottle. "What are you doing out here, in this weather? It's not safe. This is the time of predators."

His words sent a chill down my spine, but I forced a smile. I took the bottle he offered, my hands trembling and thanked him for his kindness. I tried to stand, but pain shot through my body. My knees and elbows throbbed. Seeing my struggle, the stranger reached out and helped me up, his grip firm but oddly cold.

"Careful," he said softly, helping me to my feet. "Let me take you home. It's dangerous to be out here alone."

The rain showed no signs of letting up, and the storm had turned the surrounding woods into something eerie, almost alive. Despite a voice in my head warning me to refuse, I nodded. As we walked toward his car, something felt… off. But I couldn't place it, and I was too exhausted to argue with the growing sense of unease creeping up my spine.

Just as we reached his car, an unsettling growl tore through the air. We both turned.

There, standing in the rain, was Reyansh. But this wasn't the Reyansh I knew. His eyes blazed with a fury I had never seen before. Blood dripped from the wounds I had tended to, soaking the handkerchief wrapped around them. He looked more terrifying than ever—the angel of death in his truest form. His entire presence radiated something terrifying, primal. My heart pounded in my chest, and for the first time, I was truly afraid of him.

"Leave the girl alone," Reyansh growled, his voice more feral than human. "She's with me."

The growl sent shivers down my spine. Instinctively, I grabbed the stranger's arm, my fingers trembling with fear. But when I looked at Reyansh's face, I saw something beneath the rage—a flicker of sadness, almost regret.

The stranger, seemingly unfazed, smirked. "Did you buy her? Because she's with me now. And that makes her mine." His voice slithered with something dark, his smile widening in a way that made my skin crawl. The way he looked at me felt wrong, like I was some object he had claimed.

"Don't worry, dear," he said, his grip tightening on my hand. "I'll keep you safe."

Before I could react, Reyansh lunged forward, his fist connecting with the stranger's jaw with a sickening crack. The man staggered back, blood trickling from the corner of his mouth.

"Touch her again, and I'll end you," Reyansh growled, his voice full of raw menace.

The stranger wiped the blood from his lips with the back of his hand, his eyes narrowing in a dangerous smile, but he made no further move. His unsettling calmness lingered in the air like a curse.

Reyansh grabbed my hand, pulling me away, practically dragging me along with him. I tried to resist, tried to pull away, but one sharp look from him silenced any protest. His gaze held an intensity that kept me rooted in place, a wordless command that I couldn't disobey. Despite the fear bubbling inside me, a part of me knew he wasn't going to hurt me.

The walk to my home was silent, the tension between us thick and suffocating. The rain continued to pour, each drop pounding against the earth like a drumbeat echoing our unspoken thoughts. By the time we reached my door, I was drenched, shivering from both the cold and the confusion swirling in my mind.

I unlocked the door with trembling hands, the key slipping in my fingers. As I opened the door, Reyansh's hand slid off my wrist, but just as I thought I was free, he grabbed my hand again. His grip wasn't as tight this time—almost gentle.

"Beware," he whispered, his voice soft but laced with something dark, something final. "Be safe, my love."

I looked up at him, my heart aching with too many emotions to name. But before I could respond, before I could even make sense of it all, he was gone, disappearing into the storm as quickly as he had come.

I stood there, frozen in the doorway, staring into the rain-soaked night. The wind howled, and the world around me felt just as turbulent as the storm raging inside me. Whatever this was between us—this twisted, strange connection—it wasn't over. Not by a long shot.

IX

Mornings weren't exactly my favorite part of the day, and today was no different. My rooster-shaped alarm clock had lost the snooze battle again, jarring me awake. Sunlight had already begun to spill through the window, painting my room in soft hues of gold. I groaned, realizing I was dangerously close to being late for school—again.

Rubbing the sleep from my eyes, I stumbled over to my study table, the spot where I tried to keep some order amidst the chaos of my life. After throwing on my school uniform with a speed that could rival any marathon runner, I bolted to the kitchen, grabbed the bread from the fridge, slapped some jam on it, and dashed out the door. I nibbled on my makeshift breakfast as I hurried down the street.

It had been a month since I last saw Reyansh, a month of silence, a month of regret. We hadn't spoken since that night, and every day since, I wished I could take it all back. My anger, my hasty words—everything. He had just been doing his job, something I couldn't accept in the heat of the moment. I had searched for him afterward, even returned to the barn we used to escape to, our own little world, but it was as if he had vanished. The realization stung. He might've been with me out of obligation at first, but that didn't change the fact that he had brought me back to my life. Now, all I had left was this gaping void.

As I turned down the narrow lane leading to school, the persistent blare of a car horn broke through my thoughts. I spun around, squinting against the sunlight, and saw a man leaning out of the driver's seat, waving and smiling at me. Something about him tugged at my memory, but I couldn't quite place him.

"Hey! Remember me? We met a few weeks ago—when you collapsed in front of my car, that rainy night?"

The scar near his eye, the thick brows, the thin hair—suddenly, it all clicked. That terrible night. His grin widened, but there was something unsettling about the way he looked at me. My stomach churned. I forced a smile, trying to mask my unease.

"Yeah… I remember. Thanks for helping me that night," I said cautiously.

"Hop in, I'll give you a ride to school. It's no trouble at all," he offered, his words dripping with honey.

I shook my head quickly, desperate to avoid his offer. "No, really, it's fine. School's just a short walk from here."

But he was persistent. "Come on, I'm not going to bite. I saved you that night, didn't I? Could've run you over, but I didn't."

The smile was still there, but this time it felt more like a threat than a friendly gesture. Before I could respond, he had already flung open the passenger door, beckoning me to get inside. My heart pounded. Every instinct screamed at me to run, but my feet betrayed me. I found myself stepping toward the car, my hand reaching for the door handle.

Just as I was about to get in, a voice cut through the air behind me.

"Sia! Wait!"

I spun around, my pulse still hammering, to see Meera jogging up behind me, her usual carefree smile plastered on her face. Relief washed over me like a tidal wave.

"I thought I was the only one running late today! Glad to see you'll keep me company," she beamed, waving casually at the man.

I didn't need another second to think. "Sir, I'd rather walk with my friend. Thank you for the offer," I said, forcing a strained smile before grabbing Meera's hand. Without waiting for his reply, we bolted down the street. My pulse only started to slow when we finally reached the school gate.

Panting, Meera shook her head, catching her breath. "Whoa! What was that about? I didn't know school was such a race today."

I let go of her hand, still trying to settle my nerves. "You saved me. I don't even want to think about what could've happened if you hadn't shown up."

"Saved you? From what?" she asked, eyes widening with alarm.

"Long story. I'll explain later," I muttered.

Meera shrugged but cast a wary glance behind us. I nodded, too shaken to argue.

When we finally made it to class, it was Physical Education, but Sir was on leave, which meant free time. Of course, Seema Ma'am was supposed to substitute, but she was occupied elsewhere, so we seized the opportunity to sit together and catch up on everything happening in my life. I had already filled the girls in on my argument with Reyansh. They were relieved we had parted ways, convinced it was for the best. But I had kept the accident and the creepy stranger from that night a secret—until now.

As I finished recounting the latest incident, Anaya rolled her eyes dramatically and sighed. "Honestly, Sia, someone should make a movie out of your life. You seem to attract all the chaos in the universe. First, it's a Grim Reaper, and now some strange guy from a rainy night? What's next?"

"I don't know," I admitted, rubbing my temples. "He gives me the creeps, but what if he's just a well-meaning guy? What if I'm overthinking it?"

Meera shook her head in disbelief. "Are you serious? You're still considering the possibility that he's *kind*? The guy was being a total creep, and you're confused? You're going to wait until something bad happens to believe us?"

Anaya threw her hands up in mock frustration. "We're wasting our breath here."

Digging through her bag, Anaya pulled something out and handed it to me—pepper spray. "Take this and please, for the love of all things sane, be careful. You're like family to us, Sia. Don't let your curiosity or misplaced trust get you into trouble."

I stared down at the pepper spray in my hand, a wave of warmth and security washing over me. As much as I had been through, I wasn't alone. Meera and Anaya—my lifelines, my anchors—had always been by my side, no matter how wild or unpredictable life got. With them, even the strangest days felt manageable. I couldn't help but feel a little lighter, as if their support was enough to push away the shadows.

The rest of the school day dragged on like it always did, a blur of lectures and hushed conversations. By the time the last bell rang, we were all beyond drained, practically running out of the classrooms in a desperate bid for freedom. After bidding a quick goodbye to Meera and Anaya, I started down the familiar path toward home. It was a narrow lane, the kind that was always quiet, tucked away from the main roads. Normally, I found comfort in its silence—today, though, that silence was shattered.

The screech of tires came out of nowhere, echoing against the walls of the lane. My heart leapt into my throat as I spun around, only to see a car racing toward me, much too fast. The headlights cut through the shadows like a blade, and my mind screamed at me to move—but my legs wouldn't obey. Panic locked me in place. All I could do was shut my eyes and wait for the inevitable impact. I wanted to scream, but my voice failed me, stuck behind the fear.

Then, out of nowhere, strong arms wrapped around my waist and yanked me to the side, pulling me out of the car's path in one swift movement. The world blurred around me as I was pulled against someone's chest. My breath came in sharp, ragged gasps, my body trembling from the shock.

"Shh... it's okay. I've got you," a soft voice murmured, familiar and steady.

I opened my eyes and there he was—Reyansh. His arms were still wrapped around me, holding me close as if he'd never let go. I blinked, struggling to process what had just happened. My heart was still racing, but now, it wasn't just from fear. Tears welled up in my eyes and spilled down my cheeks uncontrollably, and before I could stop myself, I collapsed into his chest, my sobs muffled against his jacket.

"Why did you leave me?" I managed to choke out between the sobs. "Do I not matter to you at all? Did I ever matter?" My voice was trembling, the hurt from all those weeks apart bubbling up to the surface.

He didn't respond immediately. He just tightened his arms around me, his chin resting gently on top of my head. His silence conveying everything that words couldn't. And yet, in that moment, his embrace was enough to calm the storm inside me.

We walked in silence after that, his arm securely around my waist, guiding me home. The chaos of my thoughts had settled, but a thousand questions still swirled in my mind. Where had he been all this time? Why had he disappeared after our argument? I had so much I wanted to say to him, to ask him—but the words seemed stuck in my throat, too heavy to speak. All I could feel was relief. Reyansh was here, with me, and that was enough for now.

As we neared my house, the familiar sight of my doorstep immediately brought me a sense of safety. But just as quickly, the relief was threatened by the idea of him leaving again. He slowed down as we reached the steps, and I could feel him preparing to step back, to leave me once more. Panic surged in my chest, and without thinking, I grabbed his arm, my voice breaking as I spoke.

"Reyansh, please... don't leave me again. I can't bear it."

His eyes softened instantly, and for a moment, they shimmered with something deep—regret, maybe, or pain. He closed the distance between us, his hands gently cradling my face as he leaned down and kissed my forehead. The gesture was tender, almost heartbreaking.

"Never," he whispered against my skin. "I can't afford to leave your side. I'll die without you."

I stared up at him, the intensity of his words sinking into me like a weight. And in that moment, it didn't matter what had happened between us before, or what mistakes we had made. The weeks of silence, the pain, the confusion—all of it faded away. What mattered was that he was here, now, with me. Whatever battles lay ahead, I knew we would face them together.

We stood there for a long while, just holding each other under the fading light of the day. I had no idea what the future held for us, but for the first time in a long time, I felt at peace. Reyansh wasn't leaving this time. And as long as he was with me, I knew I could face anything.

X

“I really cracked the code to find you,” I teased, handing Reyansh a steaming cup of coffee as I sat beside him on the plush couch. The warmth from the cup spread through my hands, and his presence truly filled the room with a calm stillness. The house no longer felt like a hollow shell. These walls, once cold and silent, now felt alive with him beside me. A part of me had feared letting him go again, terrified that he might disappear just as mysteriously as he had before. Sensing that fear, he had agreed to stay—until I was convinced he wouldn’t vanish.

“And what is this mysterious code?” he asked, before mumbling a quiet “thank you” for the coffee.

The sky outside had transformed into a fiery canvas of orange and pink as the sun bid farewell, making way for the moon. There was something serene about the way the light fell on him, highlighting the sharpness of his jaw, the calm intensity in his eyes. I couldn’t help but admire how otherworldly he looked, as if he didn’t quite belong to this world.

"Well," I began, leaning back into the cushions, "all I have to do is throw myself into a near-death experience, and *woosh*, you appear out of nowhere to save me."

I chuckled at my own joke, expecting him to laugh along, but his expression shifted. The humor drained from his face, replaced by something darker, something I didn't recognize. His hand, the one not holding the mug, curled into a fist so tightly that the knuckles turned white.

"Hey, I was just kidding," I said softly, placing my hand over his clenched fist in an attempt to calm him down. But then I noticed the glisten of tears in his eyes. One by one, they rolled down his cheek, warm drops falling onto my fingers. His pain startled me—why was he crying?

"You don't understand," he whispered, his voice barely audible over the quiet hum of the evening. "You have no idea what I've gone through these last few weeks without you. You've stirred something in me—something I can't ignore anymore. I don't want to lose you, Sia. I'd die a thousand deaths to save you. You don't deserve this fate… God is cruel for marking your life with tragedy."

His words hit me like a tidal wave, and I gently cupped his face, wiping away his tears. "Reyansh… I'm fine. I'm alive, sitting here with you. I was just joking. Don't let it get to you."

But he shook his head, as if my reassurance meant nothing. His eyes, those deep, haunted eyes, stared into mine with an intensity that made my heart clench. “You don’t get it. When I touch someone, I see things… I can see their deaths, or the deaths of the people closest to them.”

I froze, the air between us growing heavy as the realization dawned on me. His words chilled me to my core.

He took a breath, clearly hesitant to continue, but then he nodded. “The day we argued, when you walked away and I grabbed your hand… I saw it. I saw someone dying.”

“Who?” My voice was barely a whisper, dread pooling in my stomach.

“You,” he said, the single word cutting through the room like a blade.

I felt the blood drain from my face. My body turned cold, as though life itself was being sucked out of me. For a moment, I couldn’t speak. I didn’t know what to say. I had spent months wanting nothing more than to die, to escape the pain of losing my parents, but now—after finding Reyansh—everything had changed. I *wanted* to live, to live for him.

“I’ve been watching over you ever since,” Reyansh continued, his voice breaking with the weight of his confession. “This is the reason why I freaked out when I saw you with that man near the cemetery. I couldn’t let anything happen to you. After that, I kept my distance, hoping that maybe the vision wouldn’t come true. But every time I saw you, my heart ached. And every day, I feared the worst."

I swallowed hard, trying to process his words, the gravity of what he had just revealed. "So… you've been protecting me this whole time?"

"Yes," he whispered, his voice barely holding steady. "And until now, no death has touched you… but I'm terrified, Sia. I'm terrified of losing you."

The weight of his fear pressed against me, suffocating and real. I wasn't sure how to handle this new reality. All I knew was that I couldn't bear the thought of losing him either.

I looked up into his eyes, my heart racing. "Then stay," I said, my voice trembling. "Stay with me. Don't leave me. Please."

Reyansh gently pulled me closer, his arms wrapping around me like a protective shield. He kissed my forehead, his lips soft and reassuring.

"I'm never leaving your side," he promised.

***

The sun's rays peeked through the curtains, playfully dancing across my face. I groaned, pulling the blanket over my head. Why did the sun have to rise so early?

Couldn't it take a break at least for Sundays? I was on the verge of falling back into sleep's warm embrace when I heard a noise—faint clattering sounds coming from the kitchen.

A cold rush of panic shot through me, my sleepy brain jolting awake. *Who's in the kitchen?* My heart pounded in my chest as I reached for the heaviest thing within my grasp: my organic chemistry textbook. Armed with it, I tiptoed cautiously down the hallway, every step quiet and deliberate, ready to attack the intruder. But just as I was about to strike, I stopped in my tracks.

The "trespasser" was familiar.

There he stood, his broad back and chiseled muscles visible beneath his shirt, humming softly as he worked over the stove. Reyansh. I'd completely forgotten that we were now… living together. He'd been true to his word, refusing to leave my sight for fear that something might happen to me. His vision of my death—whether a curse or a blessing—I didn't know, but one thing was certain: I was grateful for every second with him.

If I were really destined to die… I thought, my heart heavy with the reality, *I'd spend every moment left with him, doing all the things I love.*

I smiled to myself, letting the warmth of that thought sink in before creeping up behind him and wrapping my arms around his waist.

"Good morning, my ray of sunshine," I mumbled against his back, inhaling the comforting scent of him.

He turned, a soft smile tugging at the corners of his lips as he enveloped me in his arms. "Morning," he said, his voice gentle. "Go freshen up. Breakfast will be ready soon."

I blinked up at him, a mix of amusement and disbelief on my face. "*You* cook?"

He chuckled, a rich, low sound that made my stomach flutter. "When you've been around for hundreds of years, you tend to pick up a few things," he teased, turning back to flip what smelled like freshly made apple pies.

I stared at him, my jaw dropping slightly. "You… you've been practicing cooking since then?"

He shrugged, as if it were the most natural thing in the world. "You have to, when life's not exactly *finite*. The world isn't static, Sia. Even after all this time, there's always something new to discover—whether it's how to make the perfect pie crust or something entirely different. I still find myself learning, just for fun."

My eyes widened, my mouth agape in amazement. "Wait… what do you mean 'hundreds of years'? How old are you exactly?"

He glanced at me, his lips quirking into a playful smile. "I've been like this for about four hundred years."

The number hit me like a truck. I stood there, speechless, trying to process the enormity of what he'd just said. Four hundred years? It didn't even seem possible. He looked so young—like he couldn't have been older than twenty-three. But four centuries?

My shock must've been evident because Reyansh chuckled again, clearly amused by my expression. "Too old for your taste?" he teased, raising an eyebrow.

I managed to find my voice, albeit shakily. "And I guess I'm too young for *your* taste. I'm not even… I mean, I'm barely an adult compared to you."

I said the words half-heartedly, the insecurity gnawing at me. Four hundred years. He must've lived lifetimes, met countless people, fallen in love hundreds of times—while I was here, experiencing my first love. The gap between us felt overwhelming.

He must have sensed my unease because he gently placed the spatula down and stepped closer. His eyes softened, filled with understanding. "Sia," he said, taking my hand in his. "Don't overthink it. What we have is ours—special and real. Let's not let doubts or time take that away from us."

His words were like a balm to my spiraling thoughts. I hugged him, feeling a sense of calm wash over me. But just as peace settled, my phone rang, shattering the moment.

I stepped away, walking to the bedroom to pick it up.

"Hello?"

There was silence on the other end, a strange static filling the line. Then, a voice, deep and chilling, cut through, deliberate and sinister. "You can't outrun what's coming, Sia. He won't be able to protect you forever."

My breath hitched. "Who... who is this?"

The line went dead.

My hands shook as I clutched the phone, my heart racing like a runaway train. Panic crawled through my veins. I rushed out of the bedroom, desperately looking for Reyansh. I found him standing in the living room, his body tense, as though he had already sensed something was wrong.

"What happened?" he asked, his voice steady, but his eyes flashed with concern.

I swallowed hard, my voice shaking as I held up the phone. "I—I just got a call… someone said you can't protect me forever."

Reyansh's expression darkened instantly. His jaw clenched, and without warning, he slammed his fist into the wall, the sound echoing through the room. My heart leaped as I rushed toward him, grabbing his hand before he hurt himself further.

"Reyansh!" I cried, holding his bruised hand. His breathing was ragged, his eyes burning with fury.

"I won't let anyone hurt you. Not while I'm here," he said, his voice low, but filled with resolve. He cupped my face with his hands, his touch gentle despite the storm raging within him. "I'll die before I let them lay a finger on you."

I gazed up at him, feeling both scared and safe at the same time. He was my protector, but there was something about this looming threat—something dark, sinister, and relentless. And deep down, I knew our fight was far from over.

But for now, as he held me close, I let myself believe that everything would be okay—at least, for a little while longer.

XI

It had been a week since that unnerving call, and though nothing had happened yet, the memory of that chilling voice haunted me. Reyansh hadn't let his guard down once; he was constantly nearby, watching over me with a quiet intensity that both comforted and unnerved me. When he had to leave, he made sure I was somewhere public—at school or with my friends—and he never let me go anywhere alone.

Today, however, things felt different.

As we settled into our seats in class, Seema Ma'am called us to attention, her tone unusually cheerful.

"So, students, we have a new member joining our class today!" she announced after taking attendance. A tall, striking girl with long curly hair tied into a ponytail and freckles dusting her cheeks stepped into the room, her presence magnetic.

"Hi, I'm Piya," she said with a confident smile. "I was in Nainital before, but I've always wanted to experience Shimla. I'm looking forward to making friends here."

The class clapped politely, and Ma'am directed her to an empty seat at the back. As she passed me, she shot me a small, friendly smile. I found myself instantly intrigued by her calm composure and warmth.

After class, my friends and I gathered around to introduce ourselves to her. Piya seemed polite and easygoing, and when she asked if I could help her catch up on notes, I happily agreed. Something about her felt refreshing, yet… strangely familiar, though I couldn't place why.

The rest of the morning dragged on with back-to-back lectures, and I was relieved when the break finally came. As we headed toward the canteen, I excused myself to go to the restroom. I usually avoided the ones at the far end of the corridor, where there were rumors of hauntings, but with the other bathrooms full, I didn't have much choice.

The corridor was eerily quiet as I stepped inside, but suddenly, I froze, hearing the faint sound of sobbing. It was a voice I recognized—Avantika's. She was always the last person I'd expect to find herself in such a vulnerable state, so hearing her quiet, anguished sobs sent a chill through me.

"Avantika?" I called softly. The crying stopped abruptly, replaced by an unsettling silence. I decided to give her some space and stepped out, making a show of letting the door close loudly so she'd think I'd left.

I waited quietly by the wall, unable to shake the feeling that something was very wrong. A few minutes later, she emerged, her face puffy, her eyes bloodshot. She seemed startled to see me, and when her gaze met mine, she quickly tried to hide her hands behind her back.

But not before I saw the bruises on her wrist, harsh and unmistakable, as though someone had struck her. Without thinking, I reached out and grabbed her arm, my heart pounding.

“Avantika, who did this to you?” I asked, my voice low but insistent.

Her face twisted with anger, and she yanked her arm out of my grasp, taking a step back. Her voice was venomous as she spat, “Get away from me, orphan. Don’t you dare touch me!”

Her words stung, but it was the look in her eyes that truly unsettled me. There was a darkness lurking there, a simmering rage I couldn’t understand.

“Don’t come near me again, Sia,” she hissed. “If you know what’s good for you, stay out of my way. Because if you don’t… I swear, I’ll make you regret it.”

The words slipped from her lips like a curse, and something cold trickled down my spine. This wasn’t the usual Avantika—a girl who enjoyed her superiority and sharp insults. This was someone different.

I stood frozen, watching her walk away, her figure fading into the shadowed corridor.

I didn't know what to say or do; Avantika's words had left me paralyzed. Her anger, her threat—it all echoed in my mind, making my head spin. I dragged myself to the table where Meera and Anaya were waiting, their usual chatter fading when they noticed my silence.

"Sia, you okay?" Meera asked, her face creased with concern.

I forced a small smile but said nothing. Avantika's words were still burning in my ears, and if I told Meera and Anaya, they'd go after her in vengeance. I wasn't sure if I wanted that. Whatever Avantika was going through felt... dangerous. But her words had hurt, and that wound was raw.

The rest of lunch passed in tense silence, my friends' glances filled with questions. Afterward, as we headed back to class, I stole a look at Avantika. She sat alone, her once-confident posture shaken, her legs trembling beneath the desk. Seeing her like that was strange—she'd always been so unflinching, almost untouchable. As much as I wanted to, I couldn't bring myself to reach out to her, not yet.

The hours dragged until the clock finally struck 3:00. I was tossing books into my bag when I noticed Avantika walking toward me, her expression uncharacteristically unsure.

"Umm... Sia," she began, her voice low. "I just... I wanted to apologize for what I said earlier. I didn't mean any of it. I was... dealing with something, and you happened to be there." She looked down, her fingers twisting nervously. "I'm sorry."

I felt Meera and Anaya's questioning eyes on me. Part of me wanted to respond, to say something reassuring, but the hurt still weighed heavily on my chest. Instead, I gave a curt nod, hoping it would be enough.

But as I turned to leave, she called out again. I turned back, surprised to see her holding out a small bottle of fruit juice, her hand trembling slightly as she extended it.

"Here," she said. "Take this as a peace offering. If you drink it, I'll know you've forgiven me."

Before I could take the bottle, Meera grabbed my arm, pulling me to a stop.

"Hold on." Meera's eyes narrowed, suspicion gleaming. "Since when does our snobby class monitor play nice? This whole 'apology' act—it doesn't suit you, Avantika. Who are you trying to fool?"

Avantika's cheeks flushed. "What's that supposed to mean?"

Anaya folded her arms, joining in. "Meera's right. It's weird. Why don't you prove it's safe and drink it yourself?"

Avantika's expression hardened, her cheeks going crimson with anger. "You people have issues no matter what I do. If I'm rude, you hate me. If I try to be nice, you hate me."

Anaya rolled her eyes. "Save it. Just keep your fake kindness to yourself."

The tension grew, and before the argument could go any further, I reached out and snatched the bottle from Meera, twisting the cap open. In one swift move, I took a long sip, half-draining it before handing it back to Avantika.

"I forgive you," I said, my voice firm. "But that's it. Let's just leave it at that, okay?"

Avantika's eyes softened, and for a moment, I saw something flicker there—something fragile, maybe even relief. But as she turned to walk away, a single tear slipped down her cheek, quickly hidden as she swiped it away with the back of her hand.

Lost in thought about Avantika, I barely registered Meera waving a hand in front of my face, pulling me back to reality. She gave me a concerned look, but I just smiled faintly, brushing it off. We walked out of the classroom together in silence, my gaze instinctively searching the hallways for any glimpse of Reyansh. But he was nowhere to be found, and an inexplicable chill crept over me.

Finally, it was time to say goodbye. After waving off Meera and Anaya, I began the quiet, solitary walk home, my mind spinning with fragments of the day—the mystery around Avantika, the strange things she'd said, and the tension that lingered between us. I hugged myself against a sudden cold breeze, trying to shake the strange sense of dread gnawing at me.

But before I could make sense of it, a wave of nausea hit me. My stomach churned violently, and my vision blurred. I stumbled, barely managing to steady myself as the world around me started spinning. Taking a shaky breath, I managed a few more steps before my legs buckled, forcing me to crouch down on the cold pavement. Darkness began to creep in around the edges of my vision, like ink seeping into water, but I could still vaguely sense what was happening around me.

Then I heard it—a loud screech of tires nearby, and the sound of hurried footsteps approaching. My pulse quickened, though my body felt heavy, paralyzed.

"Please, don't hurt her… I beg you," a voice pleaded desperately. Avantika. Her voice was thick with panic, each word punctuated by a stifled sob. "I did what you asked… please… don't harm her."

Her words were barely more than whispers, but they echoed in my mind. Who was she talking to? What was she so afraid of?

The sound of a struggle reached my ears, a dull thud as though someone had been shoved or thrown down. My heart raced as I tried to fight against the numbness that held me captive, tried to will my body to respond, but it was no use.

Then, rough hands grabbed my arm, yanking me up harshly. Pain shot through my elbow as I was lifted, and I struggled weakly, but my limbs felt heavy and unresponsive. I tried to call out, to scream, but my voice refused to cooperate.

"Let her go!" Avantika's voice broke through the haze again, choked with despair. But her protests were cut off by another sound—a soft, pained gasp as if she'd been silenced.

I felt the last threads of my consciousness slipping away as the darkness pressed in, thick and unrelenting, consuming me completely.

XII

A dull ache throbbed through my head as I blinked, trying to piece together my surroundings. Slowly, the blurry shapes of faces hovering over me came into focus—Meera, Anaya,and even Avantika, all looking down with a mixture of worry and relief. I lay on my bed, disoriented and foggy, the events that led me here swimming through my mind like half-formed memories.

"Take it easy, Sia. Just relax," Meera whispered, holding my hand gently. Her fingers brushing over my forehead in soothing strokes.

I nodded, but my eyes searched the room for one familiar figure. Finally, they landed on Reyansh, who stood by the door, his normally calm expression hardened, bruises darkening his face, and a fresh cut on his lips. His knuckles were red and raw, blood smeared across them. The sight of him, battered yet standing strong, stirred something in me. He caught my gaze, and I managed a weak smile, gesturing for him to come closer. Meera glanced at him, then stepped aside, allowing him to sit beside me.

Reyansh reached for my hand, his grip cold yet steady, though I could see a single tear slip down his cheek. He seemed to be holding back a torrent of emotions.

"I'm so sorry, Sia," he murmured, his voice trembling. "I tried—I did everything I could to protect you. I should've been there sooner. If I'd been there with you, none of this would have happened."

He looked down, his lips quivering with regret. But before I could reassure him, Avantika's voice broke through the silence, full of guilt and desperation. "It would have happened regardless. If not today, then another day," she whispered, standing at the foot of the bed, her face pale with remorse.

Anaya turned on her, anger flashing in her eyes. "You're in no position to offer advice, Avantika. Just be grateful we haven't handed you over to the police for what you did," she snapped, her tone sharp.

The tension in the room thickened, and a wave of dizziness washed over me. I winced, bringing a hand to my head, which seemed to make everyone more anxious. They instantly grew silent, their gazes filled with concern.

"It's okay, guys," I managed, my voice strained. "But I'm confused… I don't remember much. What exactly happened?"

Anaya's expression turned grim as she glanced at Meera. "Sia, you were seconds away from being kidnapped. Some guy was trying to drag you into a van just as Meera and I came back to grab our physics notes," she said, her voice tight with anger. "Just a moment later, Reyansh showed up and jumped in to help." She threw a sharp look at Avantika. "And guess what? Our so-called class monitor was part of the whole setup. That drink she gave you? It was meant to knock you out for the kidnappers' convenience."

I struggled to process her words, the reality of it settling over me like a cold shadow. Before I could respond, Avantika's shoulders began to shake, and she burst into tears, stepping closer. Reyansh moved instinctively, his protective gaze fixed on her, warning her to stay back.

"I didn't want any of this to happen, Sia," she sobbed, her voice heavy with remorse. "He was blackmailing me," she began, her voice trembling. "We met online a few weeks ago. At first, he was charming, making me feel special—like I mattered. I thought I was in love with him, so I let my guard down completely. I was so consumed by my feelings that I believed I'd do anything to keep him, even something as drastic as hurting myself to gain his approval. But then he changed. He started blackmailing me, threatening to leak my personal photos if I didn't obey him.

I was terrified, trapped. It felt like I had no choice, like I was under some kind of spell. I followed his orders without thinking about the consequences. You have to believe me," she pleaded, her eyes filled with desperation.

"But when I saw him taking you away…" her voice faltered, and tears welled up in her eyes. "Something inside me broke. I realized that if anything happened to you, I'd never forgive myself."

I could see the pain in her eyes, the guilt etched into her face. Despite the anger I felt, there was a part of me that pitied her—she'd been caught in something far darker than she'd realized.

Meera shook her head, her voice tinged with disbelief. "So, you helped him? Do you have any idea what he could have done to Sia?"

Avantika's face twisted with shame, and she nodded. "I know, I know. But I'll do anything to make it right. He's not just some guy. He's dangerous, and I wasn't thinking straight." She took a deep breath. "But I promise, I'll fight him. I won't let him hurt anyone else."

The room fell silent, and my gaze drifted to Reyansh. His jaw was clenched, his face a mask of barely contained fury. He spoke up, his voice low and resolute. "This isn't just some twisted man preying on people. Men like him… I've seen them before. Throughout history, killers have walked among us—people who feel nothing for the lives they take. I've seen firsthand the horror they leave behind."

Anaya and Meera exchanged uneasy glances, curiosity and fear evident on their faces. Reyansh continued, his voice distant, as if recalling painful memories. "I've encountered men like him numerous times—men who take pleasure in control, in fear. They're driven by something dark within them, something that feeds off others' suffering. It's people like him who leave scars on humanity."

A shiver ran down my spine as I listened, feeling the weight of Reyansh's words. My mind flashed to the bruises that I had tended to from the day I met him. His work wasn't just about taking souls; it was about facing humanity's darkest corners.

Reyansh's gaze softened as he looked back at me. "But you're safe now, and I'll do whatever it takes to keep it that way. He's out there, but he won't touch you again. I swear it."

"And you're not alone in this, Sia. We're all here to protect you," Anaya said softly, giving me a reassuring smile.

"Besides," Meera added with a mischievous grin, her eyes flicking over to Avantika, "we might even have a bait to help catch that kidnapper."

Avantika visibly flinched, glancing down as though the weight of the situation was finally pressing down on her.

"Stop scaring her, guys," I said, shifting in bed with Reyansh's steady hand helping me sit up. "First, we need to understand what he really wants. Only then can we deal with him."

I gestured to Meera to bring the first aid kit from the hall. Reyansh tried to wave it off, insisting he was fine, but I wasn't about to let him walk away from the bruises and cuts he'd earned for me. Finally, he surrendered, letting me tend to him, his eyes softening as I carefully wiped away the blood and cleaned each wound.

Soon, as the sky outside deepened to a rich indigo, my friends began to head out, each of them lingering for a moment before saying goodbye. The gravity of the day hung heavily between us, unspoken but deeply felt.

After the door closed behind them, Reyansh sat beside me, taking my hands gently in his own. His touch was cold but steadying, and as he threaded his fingers through mine, I felt a calmness settle over me.

"I got a glimpse of hell today, Sia," he whispered, his voice laced with a rare vulnerability. "The thought of losing you… I won't let it happen. As long as I'm here, I'll protect you with everything I have."

My heart softened at his words, the fierce determination in his gaze making me feel safe, even in the wake of everything that had happened. But before I could respond, a wave of exhaustion pulled me under, and I found myself slipping into a deep, restful sleep, his hand still wrapped around mine.

XIII

I blinked into the darkness, my eyes adjusting slowly. Rubbing my face, I reached out to the small table by my bed, fumbling for my phone. The screen glowed faintly, revealing the time—1:30 a.m. Night still clung to the world outside, with the moon obscured by thick clouds. A dim light spilled softly from the half-closed door, casting faint shadows into the room from the hall.

Quietly, I made my way through the door, pressing a hand to my forehead, still aching from everything that had happened. In the dim light, I saw him, slouched on the sofa, his gaze fixed somewhere on the ceiling. He looked like he was lost in the depths of his own thoughts, unaware of anything around him. I moved toward him and slid onto the sofa beside him. He looked over, slightly surprised.

Quietly, I walked over and settled beside him. He looked a bit surprised to see me.

"You haven't slept?" he asked, his voice low.

"I just woke up," I murmured, scooting closer and resting my head on his shoulder. "Saw the light on and thought I'd join you."

He laid his head gently on mine, saying nothing.

"Say something," I prompted, breaking the silence that felt like it had settled too long between us.

"What do you want to hear?" he asked.

"Anything. You've lived here for centuries—I know you have stories," I encouraged softly.

He sighed, his voice quieter, like he was remembering something distant and raw. "I existed like a virus, Sia. Always on the edge of life and death. I'd come alive only when guiding a soul to the afterlife. After that… I went back to being a ghost myself, with nothing to tether me." He paused, his hand brushing mine. "But after meeting you, I feel different—alive, like you. I have a purpose now… to protect you."

I smiled softly, my hand reaching up to brush against the cool, pale skin of his cheek. "Tell me," I murmured, "were you always a Grim Reaper? Or… did something happen?"

He glanced down, his expression clouding over with memories I could tell he had rarely, if ever, shared. "I'm not sure how to answer that," he said quietly.

"Why?" I asked, shifting so I could look into his eyes. "Is it that hard to talk about?"

A small, hesitant smile tugged at his lips as he gently guided my head back to rest on his shoulder. "Not exactly," he murmured. "It's just… I've never told anyone. No one's ever asked me to talk about it. I don't even know how to find the right words."

I traced soft circles along the back of his hand, a silent reassurance that he didn't have to tell me if he didn't want to. But after a long, drawn-out silence, he began to speak, his voice low, as if each word had to be coaxed from him.

"I remember… flames. A fire hotter than anything I've ever felt." He took a breath, his hand tightening around mine.

I looked up at him, feeling my heart pound, but his eyes were closed, lost somewhere far beyond the room, beyond us.

"When I was alive," he began, his voice a fragile whisper, "I was the son of a woman people feared. They believed my mother was a witch, a woman of dark magic, and they feared her more than anything. I didn't know much about it then—I was just a young lad of twenty. But in their eyes, her blood was tainted, and so was mine."

He paused, his jaw tightening. "I didn't realize the full weight of that fear until the night they came for us. There was a storm, and the air was thick with tension, like the earth itself was holding its breath. They dragged us both out of our house in the dead of night, bound my hands, and brought us to the center of the village. Someone had been murdered, and they believed my mother had sacrificed him for black magic. And, then… they lit a fire."

I held his hand, feeling the depth of his pain with every word he spoke.

"They burned her first. I could still hear her screams, feel the heat on my skin. I'll never forget the smell of the smoke, the sight of her face in those flames, the way her voice broke as she called out my name one last time."

His voice cracked, and I felt my chest tighten with the weight of his grief, the horror he had witnessed. He took a deep breath, steadying himself.

"After that… it was my turn. They bound me to the stake, my body pressed against the rough wood as the fire crept closer. I felt the flames licking at my skin, felt my flesh blistering, melting away in the heat. Every nerve in my body screamed for mercy, but all I could do was wait, helpless. And then, as I began to lose consciousness, I saw him."

I barely breathed, enraptured by his story. "Who?" I whispered.

"A Grim Reaper," he replied, his voice barely above a murmur. "Standing in the shadows, watching. He had come to take me, to guide my soul beyond, and in that moment of pain, I begged him to save me. To do anything to end the agony."

Reyansh's hand trembled slightly in mine, and I squeezed it gently, urging him to continue.

"But he refused," Reyansh said, his voice bitter. "He told me it was my time, that if I didn't die now, I would be left to wander as a lost soul, forever bound to this world without purpose. But the pain… it was too much. I begged, I pleaded. I would have given anything for just a few moments of relief."

A haunted look flickered in his eyes. "He turned his back on me, and I died in those flames. But when my soul rose from the ashes, I wasn't ready to let go. Anger filled every part of me, drowning out the pain, and my spirit became twisted, darkened by vengeance. I wanted them to suffer like I had. So I hunted them down, each one, the people who burned us—every last one. And they couldn't escape me, no matter where they hid."

He paused, his breath shallow. "I thought that revenge would free me. But… it only bound me more deeply to this world. I was consumed by my rage, by what I'd become. Eventually, I could no longer tell if I was a lost soul or something far worse. And that was when Death came back for me."

The room felt impossibly still, every word he spoke laden with the weight of his past.

"When I had finished my vengeance, I surrendered myself. I didn't know what awaited me. I thought maybe I'd finally get peace. But Death offered me something else: an eternity of servitude, a bond to the laws of nature. I would become one of them—a Grim Reaper."

He looked at me, his eyes dark with a complex mix of emotions: sorrow, regret, and perhaps a hint of relief for having shared this secret.

"I don't know if I'm good or bad, Sia," he said, his voice barely a whisper. "All I know is… this is who I am now."

I lifted my hand, brushing my fingers across his cheek, wanting to ease even a fraction of the pain that lingered in his gaze. The man before me had been forged in fire and vengeance, his soul bound by a dark and complex past. But to me, he was more than a Grim Reaper, more than a creature of darkness.

"You're not just what happened to you, Reyansh," I whispered, letting my hand linger on his face. "You're so much more."

I held him tightly, as if weaving together the fragments of his soul, yearning to mend the scars that ran deeper than skin. He embraced me back, his arms encircling me like a protective cocoon, grounding us in this fragile moment.

"Since that day," he began, his voice a soft caress, "I've been tethered to the laws of life and death. I can't disrupt the natural order. My purpose is to shepherd souls to the afterlife. I've encountered gentle spirits, but I've also faced fierce, vengeful ones—echoes of my own past. It's no small feat to capture them. Outside the body, they possess an unearthly power, liberated from the shackles of mortality. They are nearly invincible, untouched by the ailments of the flesh."

His voice dipped, a sigh escaping his lips, laced with memories. "The wounds you saw on me when we first met—and in the days that followed—were marks from my struggles with those defiant souls, the ones who cling to this world with a desperate ferocity."

I remembered every moment I'd discovered him injured, every silent plea etched in his expression. The world around us hushed, a sacred silence enveloping us as I held him closer, a vow whispered in my embrace: *I am here for you, always.*

"Do you know," he murmured, his gaze drifting into the distance, "when I met your parents… it was the first time I ever shed tears. I questioned how God could inflict such cruelty on a heart as pure as yours." He paused, the weight of his words hanging in the air. "Yet, all I could do was stand by and watch."

I pulled away slightly, needing to meet his eyes as he spoke of my parents. His gaze softened, shimmering with a tenderness that broke my heart.

"They were two of the kindest souls I've ever known," he said, his voice rich with emotion. "Their only request was simple: to watch over you, to ensure you'd never feel alone and that no harm would befall you."

Tears spilled from my eyes, and he reached up, his cool fingers brushing them away with unexpected gentleness. He pressed a soft kiss to my forehead, the warmth of his breath igniting something within me.

"And that day," he whispered, "when you questioned whether I was with you out of pity…"

I placed my fingers over his lips, silencing the shadows of doubt. "Please, no more," I urged, my heart racing.

But he held my hand, lowering it gently, his grip firm yet tender. "I need to say this," he insisted.

His eyes locked onto mine, a fierce tenderness radiating from him. "There was so much I left unsaid. When I first laid eyes on you, your kindness ensnared my heart. When I realized I would be the one to take your parents from you, sadness enveloped me. But it was more than that—I felt an empathy so profound. I, too, have lost my parents. I understood that depth of pain." He paused, his words crafted with care, as if each syllable was a brushstroke on the canvas of our connection. "Yet, the more time I spent with you, the more I found myself ensnared by your light. My affection blossomed into something undeniable. I fell deeply in love with you, Sia. Now, each moment apart feels like an eternity, a void of lifelessness."

His confession wrapped around me like a warm blanket, igniting a spark within my heart. Unable to contain my emotions, I leaned in, resting my forehead against his, the coolness of his skin a soothing balm against my warmth. Our breaths intertwined, creating a soft melody, a rhythm only we could hear.

"You have no idea what you mean to me, Reyansh. You must know, right here and now." I closed my eyes, letting the truth spill forth like a river breaking free from its dam. "I am hopelessly, irrevocably in love with you."

In that dimly lit room, the air shimmered with unspoken promises, and a lullaby of love enveloped us. In that moment, nothing else existed—just the two of us, bound together by the fragile threads of fate, our hearts beating in perfect harmony.

XIV

I was jolted out of my trance by a cacophony of shouts and squeals. The classroom had erupted into chaos—girls darting around, clustering by the windows, their voices rising in excitement. For a moment, I couldn't place where I was. My thoughts had been elsewhere, drifting in a fog that had settled over me ever since *that* incident.

It felt like a lifetime ago, though in reality, not much time had passed. Life had seemingly returned to normal—at least on the surface. Nothing strange has happened since, as if that day had been nothing more than a vivid dream. But deep inside, I wasn't the same. My mind felt like a cluttered attic, crammed with thoughts I couldn't sort. Overthinking wasn't new for me, but now? Now, I felt like I was constantly teetering on the edge of some invisible precipice, zoning out more often than usual.

As my awareness settled back into the classroom, I noticed Avantika stride in. Her presence was as commanding as ever, her voice cutting through the noise with the authority only she seemed to possess.

"Due to this terrible weather, no one is allowed to leave alone," she announced, her tone clipped and matter-of-fact. "Messages have already been sent to your parents. You're only permitted to leave campus once they arrive."

The room erupted in a collective groan of disappointment. Some girls sighed dramatically, others muttered their complaints under their breath. The noise began to die down as the crowd at the windows dispersed, revealing what had captured everyone's attention.

The world outside had transformed. Snowflakes danced and swirled against the window panes, tiny white crystals clinging to the glass. They sparkled softly, their delicate beauty a stark contrast to the gray skies beyond.

For reasons I couldn't quite explain, watching the snow fall eased the weight in my chest. A faint, fleeting sense of peace fluttered in my heart, as if the snow was whispering a quiet reminder: even amidst the storms—both outside and within—there was still beauty to be found.

After making her announcement, Avantika slowly made her way toward me. Her expression was unusually soft, almost... caring.

"You don't need to worry, Sia," she said, her voice uncharacteristically gentle. "I've already spoken to my dad. We'll drop you home."

I managed a small smile. It wasn't the first time she'd offered to help. Ever since *that* incident, Avantika had become unrecognizably kind—too kind, almost. It was as if guilt had carved its way into her conscience, and now she was determined to make amends. She had taken it upon herself to hover around me, playing the role of an overprotective friend.

Even Anaya and Meera had started growing impatient with her unrelenting niceness. I didn't have the heart to tell her to back off, though. Something about her efforts felt genuine, even if they were overwhelming.

"Thanks, Avantika," I said politely, "but Reyansh is coming to pick me up. I'll wait for him. Still, I appreciate it."

Her expression faltered for a split second, disappointment clouding her features before she nodded curtly. "Alright," she murmured, stepping away without another word.

One by one, the crowd of girls began to thin out as parents arrived to take their daughters home. The classroom grew quieter, leaving just a handful of us behind. I drifted to the window, drawn to the delicate dance of snowflakes outside. Their intricate patterns clung to the glass, each one unique, each one fleeting.

Anaya wasn't here today—she'd been bedridden with a fever—and Meera had left for her village to be with her ailing grandmother. For the first time in what felt like ages, I was truly alone.

"Want to come with me, Sia?" a quiet voice interrupted my thoughts.

I turned to see Pia standing behind me. Over the past few weeks, we had somehow transitioned from strangers to friends, though she was nothing like my other friends. Pia was reserved, observant, and spoke only when she felt it was necessary.

"I think I'll wait," I replied. "Someone's coming to get me."

Pia nodded, her expression unreadable. I hadn't confided in her about Reyansh yet—our friendship hadn't reached that level of trust.

"I doubt he'll make it today," she said, shrugging casually as she headed for the door. "Being a Grim Reaper isn't exactly an easy job."

Her words stopped me cold. My heart skipped a beat, and my mouth fell open in shock. How did she know about Reyansh? And about... *that?*

I stood frozen, my mind racing. By the time I regained my senses and bolted after her, Pia was already gone, leaving me alone with a storm of questions swirling in my head.

The hours after that felt like a whirlwind, my mind trapped in a constant tug-of-war with a single question: *How did Pia know about Reyansh?* Aside from Meera and Anaya, who would never share his secret, no one else knew. Pia's cryptic remark rattled me more than I cared to admit.

By the time I snapped out of my spiraling thoughts, the classroom was empty. Even the remaining few lingering students had gone, leaving only the security guard pacing impatiently by the door. The clock read 5:00 PM. I sighed, grabbed my bag, and left the room. The snowfall had paused, leaving the air crisp and still. Reyansh's absence gnawed at me. He was never late—*never*. Pia's words echoed in my mind, each syllable twisting the knot of unease in my stomach.

I wandered aimlessly down the now-cleared road, the neatly shoveled heaps of snow glowing faintly in the streetlights. My steps faltered when I saw a familiar figure standing by the roadside in our school uniform. My heart skipped a beat.

It was Pia.

And next to her, lying on the ground in a pool of crimson-streaked snow, was a figure that made my blood run cold. Reyansh.

My legs moved before my brain could catch up. I sprinted toward them, dropping to my knees beside him and cradling his head in my lap. His face was pale, and blood oozed from wounds across his body. My hands trembled as I called his name, my voice cracking with desperation.

Pia stood nearby, utterly unbothered, her expression eerily calm. "I told you," she said flatly. "Being a Grim Reaper isn't an easy job."

Her detached tone hit me like a slap. This wasn't the Pia I knew—the quiet, composed girl who was always ready to help. Standing there, she felt like a stranger, cold and unrecognizable. I wanted to scream at her, to demand answers, even punch her smug face. But right now, Reyansh was all that mattered.

"Help me take him home," I pleaded, my voice shaking.

Pia glanced at her watch as if she had all the time in the world. "The second car that passes will be Avantika's. She stopped for coffee before heading on her way home. You'll see her in five minutes. Ask for her help."

She turned and walked away, leaving me staring after her, dumbfounded and seething. The absurdity of her statement infuriated me—what kind of person delivers riddles instead of help? Yet, a small part of me wanted to believe her. She knew about Reyansh, after all.

Two minutes passed, and then a white car slowed to a stop beside us. A man, probably in his early thirties, rolled down the window and asked if I needed help. I hesitated, then shook my head. He insisted, but I managed to wave him off. No sign of a second car. Three minutes. I started cursing myself for trusting Pia when, at last, a red car pulled up.

The window rolled down, revealing Avantika clutching a takeout coffee cup. She squealed in shock when she saw me and bolted out of the car, her father—a tall, lean man with a neatly trimmed mustache—following close behind.

"Avantika, please!" I begged, tears streaming down my face. "Say no more. Just take us home. Please."

Her panic mirrored my own as her father assessed the situation. Together, they helped me lift Reyansh's limp body into the backseat. Avantika's father wanted to take him to a hospital, but I refused, insisting on taking him home. His wounds heal fast and it would only raise questions.

Once home, Avantika and her father helped me carry Reyansh to my room and settle him on the bed. His wounds were gruesome—deep gashes on his head, a bloody tear along his waist, and countless scratches marring his pale skin. My hands worked mechanically, cleaning and bandaging the injuries as best as I could. All the while, questions burned in Avantika's wide eyes, mirroring her father's concerned gaze.

"I'm sorry for not offering you a proper welcome," I murmured after finally finishing the first aid. "Thank you for everything."

They brushed off my apology, their worry etched into their faces. "Take care of yourself, Sia," Avantika's father said before they left.

The door clicked shut behind them, and I was finally alone. My gaze lingered on Reyansh, his chest rising and falling with shallow breaths. I knelt by his side, brushing his hair back gently. The weight of the day pressed down on me, but there was no time for tears. Not yet.

"Stay with me," I whispered. "Please don't leave."

The snow began to fall again, silent and unyielding, as if the world itself had paused to watch.

XV

I hadn't realized when I'd dozed off, my body slouched awkwardly on the bed beside him. My right hand rested lightly on his chest, rising and falling with his shallow breaths, while my left hand supported my tilted head. It wasn't until I felt him stir beneath me that I woke, startled and filled with panic.

"Are you alright?" I asked quickly, my voice trembling with worry. "I was so scared. Tomorrow, we're getting you a phone. Enough of this weird telepathy thing—this is the 21st century, for heaven's sake!" The words spilled out of me in a flurry of nonsensical rambling as he tried to sit up, wincing in pain.

"Stop moving!" I scolded gently, pressing him back down onto the pillow. "I'll get you anything you need. Just stay still, please."

His eyes locked onto mine, intense yet soft, and I felt the heat rise in my cheeks. He didn't say anything, just stared at me with that look that made my heart flutter uncontrollably.

"Stop looking at me like that," I mumbled, pulling the blanket over him to avoid his gaze.

"But why?" he asked, his voice laced with innocent curiosity. His hand reached up to tuck a loose strand of hair behind my ear, the light brush of his fingers sending a shiver down my spine.

I blinked, surprised that he had heard my whispered complaint. "Your stare… it makes me nervous," I admitted, my voice barely above a whisper.

"Why?" he asked again, his tone playful, as if he enjoyed watching me squirm.

I hesitated, then confessed, "Whenever you look at me like that—with so much... love—I don't know how, but butterflies go wild in my stomach."

The words had barely left my lips when my stomach betrayed me with a loud, embarrassing grumble. My cheeks flushed crimson, and I wished the earth would swallow me whole.

Reyansh stared at me for a second before bursting into laughter, the sound deep and rich, echoing through the room. But his laughter quickly turned to wincing as he clutched his side, the pain from his injuries cutting his amusement short.

"This big reaction couldn't be just because of my gaze," he teased, a mischievous glint in his eyes.

I smacked his chest playfully. "You should know, Mr. Grim Reaper, that I haven't eaten anything since lunch at 12:30. Unlike you, I'm human and need food to survive."

He chuckled, then tried to sit up again. "What would you like? I'll make it for you."

"Absolutely not!" I pushed him back down firmly, my hands on his shoulders. "You need rest."

Before I could say more, he looked at me with exaggerated seriousness. "Are you always this stubborn, or is it just for me?"

"Only for you," I shot back, crossing my arms. "Someone has to keep you in check."

His laughter returned, softer this time, and his hand reached out to ruffle my hair. "Alright, boss. I'll stay put."

It was strange—seeing him like this. For the first time since I'd met him, Reyansh was relaxed, carefree, even joking. The usual weight of his responsibilities seemed to lift, if only for a moment. And despite my embarrassment, I couldn't help but smile.

I wandered into the kitchen and pulled out a packet of oats. It was late, and the last thing I wanted was to exhaust myself—or him—by making something elaborate. Within minutes, I had a steaming bowl ready and hurried back to the room, my mind buzzing with unanswered questions.

When I entered, I found him sitting upright on the bed, his back resting against the headboard. His face lit up with a wide, unguarded smile. It stopped me in my tracks. I couldn't remember ever seeing him smile like that before—not so openly, not so… humanly.

I sat down beside him on a chair, holding the bowl. Scooping up a spoonful of oats, I brought it to his lips. He accepted it without protest, his gaze never leaving mine.

"I hope you remember I'm a Grim Reaper," he teased softly after a few bites. "More than me, you're the one who needs food to survive. Eat."

I hesitated, wanting to insist that he finish the bowl, but I knew better. He didn't need the food like I did, and my grumbling stomach earlier was proof enough that I had to take care of myself too. So, with a small nod, I ate the rest, finishing it quickly before rushing back to his side.

This time, instead of sitting in the chair, I hesitated near the bed. He patted the space beside him, silently asking me to sit next to him again. My heart raced as I complied, sinking onto the mattress, my hands nervously twisting the hem of my shirt.

He shifted closer, his movements careful and deliberate. Slowly, his arm reached around my shoulders, guiding me to rest my head against his chest. I stiffened for a moment before relaxing into him, the steady rhythm of his heartbeat merging with my own frantic one.

For a while, we stayed like that, wrapped in a silence that felt like the world had paused for us. It was comforting, grounding, and for the first time that day, I felt like everything might be okay.

"Reyansh?" I whispered tentatively.

He let out a soft hum, resting his chin gently on top of my head.

"Do you want to tell me how you ended up like this?" I asked, my voice barely audible.

He sighed, the sound carrying a mix of exhaustion and resignation. "It was nothing unusual," he began. "Just another vengeful soul. He was more powerful than most I've dealt with, though—unrelenting, dangerous."

I stayed quiet, urging him to continue.

"For a moment, I thought about letting him be—letting him do whatever he wanted. But something stopped me. I couldn't give up. I forced myself to fight back and finally captured him." His tone shifted slightly, a hint of pride seeping through. "For the first time in a while, I felt proud of myself."

"That's why you're so happy?" I asked softly, looking up at him.

He nodded, his voice low and steady. "Yes. Because if I can handle a soul that strong, I know I'll be able to deal with whoever—or whatever—is after you. I want to be strong for you, Sia. I need to protect you."

My chest tightened, and I pulled back just enough to look at him. My eyes burned with unshed tears, and I struggled to hold them back. The weight of his words settled over me like a blanket, warm and heavy. How deeply did he love me, that he was willing to bear so much pain just to keep me safe?

He must have noticed the emotion in my gaze because he leaned forward and pressed a soft kiss to my forehead. The moment felt infinite, like time had stretched to accommodate the quiet intensity between us.

When he pulled back, I remembered something that had been nagging at me since earlier. "Reyansh… do you know anything about Pia?" I asked cautiously.

His brow furrowed slightly. "Only what you've told me. Why? Did something happen?"

"Nothing you need to worry about," I said quickly, avoiding his questioning gaze as I ducked my head back against his chest.

He already had so much to deal with. Whatever Pia's intentions were, I'd figure them out on my own. For now, all that mattered was that we were here together, and for the first time in what felt like forever, the world outside didn't matter.

XVI

The shrill crow of my rooster alarm shattered the morning quiet, pulling me from a haze of dreams. Still half-asleep, I groaned and began patting the bed aimlessly, trying to locate the offending noise. My fingers met only soft fabric, and the alarm kept blaring, relentless and mocking.

With a frustrated sigh, I cracked open my eyes—and immediately froze. My head was resting on his chest, his steady heartbeat beneath my ear. Blood rushed to my cheeks, painting them a deep crimson. Everything else faded into the background, even the piercing squawk of the rooster alarm.

Hesitantly, I reached out and traced my fingertips along his forehead, then down the bridge of his nose. My fingers lingered briefly on his lips, before trailing down to his chin. His features were flawless, even in sleep—too perfect, too unreal.

A soft groan escaped his lips, and his hand shot up, catching mine. His grip was firm but warm as he placed my hand on his chest, holding it there as though it belonged. “For heaven’s sake, Sia,” he muttered, his voice thick with sleep. “Turn off that infernal rooster.”

I bit back a giggle, stifling my amusement as I shuffled across the bed. After a moment of searching, I finally found my phone nestled near the edge by my feet. With a triumphant tap, the rooster was silenced, leaving the room in peaceful quiet once more.

The spell of the moment broke, and I realized the time. I needed to get ready. Careful not to wake him, I slipped out of bed and tiptoed across the room, grabbing my uniform along the way.

The warm water of the shower did little to calm the fluttering butterflies in my stomach. By the time I slipped into my school uniform, I couldn’t tell if my flushed cheeks were from the heat or the lingering memory of Reyansh’s touch.

The mouthwatering aroma wafting from the kitchen pulled me from my thoughts, a sure sign that Reyansh was awake and, as always, one step ahead of me. Slinging my bag over my shoulder, I made my way to the kitchen, where the dining table was already set with a steaming cup of coffee and a plate of golden-brown sandwiches. My lunchbox, neatly packed, sat nearby, all thanks to him.

He was at the stove, humming a soft lullaby under his breath, the melody unfamiliar but oddly soothing. His wounds were gone now, completely healed, as if the events of the previous day were nothing more than a bad dream.

I slid into my seat and began eating, savoring the comforting flavors. Reyansh joined me, settling into the chair beside mine, resting his chin on his hand as he gazed at me intently.

"What?" I asked, pausing mid-bite.

"Nothing," he replied, a playful glint in his eyes. "I just like looking at you."

My cheeks burned at his bluntness, and I shook my head, focusing on my breakfast instead. I needed all the energy I could muster to face Pia today. The thought of her twisted my stomach—not from butterflies, but from unease. It stung to realize how badly I'd misjudged her. I'd thought we were on the path to becoming friends, but I'd been so wrong.

When I finished eating, Reyansh shrugged on his long, warm coat to walk me to school. The snow had stopped, and the sun shone brightly, making the remaining heaps of snow along the roadside sparkle like scattered diamonds. The scene was almost too perfect to belong to the kind of day I knew awaited me.

At the school gates, I turned to him, offering a small wave. "Thanks for walking me," I said.

"Always," he replied, his tone soft but steady.

I took a deep breath and stepped inside, steeling myself for the confrontation I dreaded. Pia.

I quickened my pace toward the classroom, bracing for the sight of her. But when I reached the door, her chair was empty. My heart sank. Pia was always early—this was the first time in a month that she wasn't in her seat.

A chill ran through me, and not from the weather. *Is she avoiding me?* The thought made my stomach churn. Was she deliberately hiding to dodge my questions?

I made my way to my desk, the absence of Anaya and Meera feeling sharper than ever. Both were still on leave. They wouldn't be back until Monday.

Today was Friday. Just one day to get through alone. Then, two days at home to collect my thoughts. And come Monday, I'd finally have them back by my side.

But until then, I had to face this on my own.

I sighed, pulling out my English literature textbook as the first lecture of the day was about to begin. Sunaina Ma'am entered the room, her sharp gaze sweeping over the class before she began calling out attendance. My heart sank when she reached Pia's name. Hearing it felt like a cruel reminder of my failure. I had come to school today with one goal: to confront her. But she wasn't here.

Sunaina Ma'am called her name again, and just as I resigned myself to another day of unanswered questions, a familiar, soft voice answered from the doorway. "Present, Ma'am."

Pia's polite tone was the same as always, but it sent a shiver down my spine. Sunaina Ma'am frowned at her tardiness but waved her in. Pia slipped into her seat without so much as a glance in my direction, her calm demeanor making my frustration bubble over.

I couldn't focus on a single word of the lecture. My eyes stayed glued to her, my mind racing with the questions I had been rehearsing for hours. As soon as the bell rang, signaling the end of class, I sprang to her desk.

"We need to talk," I said firmly, my voice low but insistent.

Pia didn't even look up. Instead, she calmly pulled a water bottle from her bag, took a sip, and placed it back as though I wasn't standing right there.

"Pia," I said again, my patience wearing thin.

She finally turned her cool gaze to me, her lips curling into a faint, detached smile. "Relax, Sia. I'm not going to run away. It's usually people like you who try to escape me."

Her cryptic words only fueled my frustration. Before I could demand an explanation, Jaiveer Sir entered the classroom for physics. I groaned inwardly as the lecture began, trapping me in my seat and keeping my questions locked in my head.

By the time the bell rang for lunch, I turned toward Pia's seat, ready to finally get my answers—but she was gone. Panic gripped me as I scanned the room, then bolted out the door. My eyes darted around the corridors until I spotted her on the secluded staircase leading to the auditorium.

She sat there, perfectly composed, as though she had been waiting for me. Without looking back, she patted the step beside her, gesturing for me to sit. I hesitated but obeyed, settling down beside her in tense silence.

Before I could begin, she broke it. "So, Sia," she said, her voice unnervingly calm. "What's it like to fall in love with a being who isn't even human?"

Her words hit me like a punch to the gut. I stiffened, my voice barely steady as I asked, "How do you know about him?"

She tilted her head slightly, her expression unreadable. "Does it really matter?"

"Yes," I replied firmly, gathering every ounce of courage I had. "It matters. Who are you, Pia? And how do you know about Reyansh?"

She let out a dry, humorless laugh, her eyes glinting with something cold. "I expected more from you, Sia. Instead, you're wasting time with irrelevant questions."

"Then tell me," I pressed. "What questions should I be asking?"

Her smile faded, replaced by an expression so serious it made my chest tighten. "You and Reyansh are defying the laws of nature, and you think you'll get away with it?" Her voice was sharp, cutting through the air like a blade. "Do you even realize the consequences of what you're doing? Playing with fire always comes with a deep burn."

My throat went dry. I had never thought about it that way before, never considered the weight of what we were risking. "What do you mean?" I whispered, dread creeping into my voice.

Pia reached into her pocket and pulled out a pen. Grabbing my hand, she wrote a single, elegant number across my palm: 2.

I stared at the number, my brows furrowing in confusion. "What does this mean?"

She met my gaze, her tone cold and unyielding. "You have two days. You should have died already, but Reyansh broke the rules to save you. Now, there's no more time to spare. In two days, either you must die, or he will. Life and death cannot fall in love, Sia. It's a ridiculous notion, and nature will not allow it."

Her words sent a chill through me, freezing me in place. "What... what are you saying?" I stammered.

She stood, brushing off her trousers as she prepared to leave. "It's simple. Only one of you can survive this battle. You need to decide: who will it be?"

Her words echoed in my ears, leaving me reeling as she turned to walk away. Summoning every ounce of strength I had, I called after her. "Pia! Who are you?"

She stopped, half-turning with a smirk that chilled me to my core. "You'll figure it out soon enough," she said. And then, she vanished into thin air, leaving nothing but the faint echo of her laughter behind.

I sat there, my heart pounding and my mind spinning with the weight of her words. Two days. A choice. And a truth I was nowhere near ready to face.

XVII

Pia's words played on a loop in my mind as the final bell rang. I gathered my things and headed toward the school gate, lost in my own tangled thoughts. As usual, Reyansh was waiting for me, leaning casually against the gate. The sight of him should have brought me comfort, but today, it only added to the weight pressing on my chest.

I managed a meek smile as I approached him, though my heart wasn't in it. He raised an eyebrow, clearly picking up on my strange demeanor. I shook my head quickly, hoping he wouldn't ask questions. Without a word, he reached out to take my bag, his movements calm and familiar.

Just as we turned to head home, Pia's voice stopped me in my tracks.

"Sia, Seema Ma'am asked me to give you this practical file," she said, holding out the neatly bound file. "She's checked it."

Her tone was light, her demeanor perfectly normal. If I hadn't had that chilling conversation with her earlier, I might have believed this was the real Pia.

Before I could respond, she turned her attention to Reyansh, her smile widening. "Long time no see. It's good to see you... *Reyansh*," she said, her voice laced with emphasis on his name.

I felt him stiffen beside me. He didn't respond, his silence unnerving. Pia simply waved goodbye and walked away, her figure disappearing into the snowy street.

I watched her go, my thoughts swirling. How could one person switch so seamlessly between normal and inexplicable so effortlessly? She was a mystery I couldn't unravel.

Reyansh, still rooted to the spot, muttered, "Why is she here?" His voice was distant, almost as if he were speaking to himself.

"You know her?" I asked, my curiosity piqued. "When I brought her up before, you denied knowing anything about her."

He nodded, though his movements were mechanical. "Is this Pia? The one you were talking about?"

My head spun with questions. "Wait, you just said you know her. How could you not know her name?"

He said nothing, his silence heavy with something unspoken. Without another word, we began walking home. The tension between us was palpable, and though I desperately wanted answers, I didn't push. Reyansh wasn't ready to talk.

When we got home, I changed into something more comfortable, trying to shake off the chill of the snow that had started falling again. The weather had returned to its icy, crystalline beauty, and I found myself craving warmth. I headed to the kitchen and quickly made two mugs of coffee, the rich aroma filling the air.

Carrying the steaming mugs, I found Reyansh standing by the window, his gaze fixed on the falling snow. The world outside seemed still, almost magical, as the delicate crystals drifted from the sky. He looked lost in his thoughts, his expression faraway and unreadable.

I nudged him gently, handing over the mug of coffee. His fingers brushed mine briefly, sending a tiny spark through me, but his attention remained fixed on the falling snow outside. The soft rustling of the wind filled the silence between us, heavy with unspoken questions.

I couldn't hold it in any longer. "Reyansh," I began, my voice soft but insistent, "I need to ask you something."

He shifted slightly, his posture tightening, but his gaze didn't leave the snow. "What is it?"

"How do you know Pia?" I asked carefully.

For a moment, he glanced at me, his dark eyes unreadable, before returning his attention to the snowy landscape. A deep sigh escaped him.

"Did she say something to you? Something… odd?" he asked, his tone calm but probing.

"No," I lied, shaking my head. "Who is she?" I pressed, lowering my voice as if afraid of the answer.

This time, he turned to face me fully, his expression serious. "Destiny," he said simply.

I frowned, confusion swirling in my mind. "I don't understand."

He sighed again, his shoulders sagging slightly, before moving to sit on the couch. He gestured for me to join him, and I sank into the seat beside him, the warmth of his presence calming yet brimming with tension.

"She is our destiny," he began slowly. "Think of her as the architect of our lives—yours and mine. Every moment we've lived, every choice, every twist of fate... it's all been designed by her. She's the writer of our story."

I stared at him, stunned. The idea that someone could shape lives like this, like a divine author, was both fascinating and overwhelming.

"So, is she just my destiny? Or does she guide everyone's lives?" I asked, my curiosity sharpening.

"She's yours," he said with a faint smile, "and she's mine too. We share the same destiny because we're intertwined. Our fates are bound together."

His words settled over me like a blanket of wonder. "Every destiny is born the moment a baby is conceived," he explained. "They become the guardian and fate of not just the child, but their future soulmate. If Pia has appeared to us both, it means she's our destiny. We're soulmates, Sia."

The air seemed to shift around us, the weight of his words filling the room. I thought back to the first time I met him. "That's why you looked so familiar to me," I murmured.

He nodded. "It's the connection between us. Two halves of a whole, drawn together, constantly seeking completion."

"That's why I feel… complete when I'm with you," I whispered, my voice trembling with emotion. He smiled softly and pressed a kiss to my forehead, his warmth spreading through me.

I hesitated before asking the next question, my voice barely above a whisper. "So… how do you know her? Have you met her before?"

His smile faded slightly, replaced by a distant look. "Kind of, yes," he admitted. "It was years ago, at the same cemetery where we first met. Back then, I was newly appointed as the Grim Reaper. I didn't fully understand my role, and the burden of it all was… crushing."

He paused, his voice growing softer. "It was midnight, and I wasn't expecting anyone else to be there. But then she appeared. She looked the same then as she does now, like time hasn't touched her. She approached me, and without a word, she healed my wounds. Then, she spoke a prophecy…"

Reyansh's words hung in the air, fragile and weighty, as he hesitated. His gaze met mine, and for the first time, I saw something unguarded in his eyes—something I couldn't quite place.

I leaned closer, my heart racing. "What prophecy, Reyansh?" I asked, my voice calm despite the storm brewing inside me.

He hesitated a moment longer before speaking, his voice quiet but deliberate. "She said, 'Someday, you will meet a young woman at this very spot. She will heal all your wounds.'"

I stared at him, struggling to process his words. My mind churned, grappling with the impossibility of it all. It felt too surreal, too far beyond what I thought I understood about the world.

Reyansh's words lingered between us, a fragile truth that seemed to shift the very air in the room. His voice, though quiet, carried the weight of something deeply personal, something he had carried alone until now.

I searched his face, the flicker of vulnerability there breaking down the walls I hadn't realized he'd built. For the first time, Reyansh didn't seem untouchable, like the powerful Grim Reaper I'd come to know. He looked human—achingly so.

And yet, his words unsettled me. The idea that my presence in his life had been foretold, that my role was to heal wounds I didn't fully understand, left me feeling both honored and unworthy.

"Reyansh," I whispered, the knot in my chest tightening. "Do you really believe that's me? That I'm… that person?"

He turned his gaze to me, his eyes softening. "I don't believe it, Sia," he said, his voice trembling slightly. "I know it. You've already started healing me. From the moment I met you, everything changed. You've made me feel things I didn't think I could anymore—hope, warmth, even joy. For someone like me, that's not just rare. It's a miracle."

My breath caught, tears pricking at the corners of my eyes. "I don't know if I can live up to that," I admitted, my voice barely audible. "What if I'm not enough?"

He reached out then, his hand gently cupping my cheek. His touch was warm, steady. "You already are," he said firmly, his eyes locking onto mine. "You don't have to do anything, Sia. Just being here, as you are… that's enough."

For a moment, I couldn't speak. The storm inside me calmed, replaced by a warmth I couldn't describe. In that instant, I realized how deeply our lives, our fates, were intertwined—and how terrifyingly beautiful that was.

Reyansh's words settled over me like a warm blanket, his steady gaze anchoring me amidst the whirlwind of emotions. For a while, neither of us spoke, the silence between us comfortable yet charged. The weight of his confession lingered, and though his words brought me a sense of peace, they also left me with a thousand unspoken questions.

I looked down at my hands, my fingers lightly tracing the edge of my coffee mug. "It's a lot to take in," I admitted softly. "This… prophecy, you, Pia—it's like stepping into a world I never knew existed."

Reyansh leaned back slightly, his expression thoughtful. "That's exactly what it is—a world you weren't meant to know about until now. The connection between us, Sia… it's more than fate. It's a thread that ties us together across realms, across lifetimes. And now that you're aware of it, things will only get more complicated."

I nodded, trying to absorb his words, though they only seemed to deepen the mystery. My mind swirled with questions that I couldn't quite put into words. Finally, I asked, "Does it ever get easier? Understanding all of this, I mean?"

He smiled faintly, his gaze distant. "Not really. The more you learn, the more questions you have. Even for someone like me, there's so much I don't know."

His honesty grounded me somehow, reminding me that even beings like him weren't all-knowing. But curiosity still burned within me, refusing to be silenced. "Why do all these celestial beings take human form?" I asked suddenly, the question bursting out before I could stop it.

At my question, Reyansh burst into a sharp laugh that startled me. "What if she met you in the form of a goat? Would you have understood her words then?" he said, his tone teasing.

I couldn't help but crack a smile at his absurd example, though it faded as he continued.

"All celestial beings are formless. They're pure energy—vast, shapeless, and intangible. Even Grim Reapers are just energy at their core, but they operate at levels far beyond human understanding. I only exist in human form because I wasn't originally a Grim Reaper. I became one after my death," he explained, his voice calm but tinged with something deeper.

I tilted my head, my curiosity growing. "That's fascinating. So… how does this whole celestial system work?"

Reyansh gave me a small, wry smile. "The universe is vast, Sia. Far beyond what you can imagine—or even what we celestial beings can fully comprehend. We operate on something like an instinct, a flow of telepathic energy that guides us in our tasks. It's not entirely different from the intuition humans feel. But how the universe truly functions… that's a mystery even to us."

His words carried an air of awe and humility, a rare glimpse into the uncertainty that even beings like him faced.

I nodded, letting his words sink in, though they only seemed to unleash more questions than answers. The world felt infinitely larger now, the boundaries of what I thought I knew stretching far beyond their limits.

"But always listen to her," Reyansh said, his voice low but firm. "Every word she speaks is the truth. She will never misguide you. She is your destiny, Sia. Treat her words as sacred, like the word of God."

His seriousness rooted me in place, my thoughts spiraling back to my earlier conversation with Pia. Her cryptic warnings suddenly carried a heavier weight. It was true—her words were a testimony of fate. And the decision she'd left me with was no mere illusion.

One of us had to die.

The realization struck like a lightning bolt, and I felt the blood drain from my face. A choice that would determine life and death—and I had just two days to make it.

Reyansh nudged me gently, his worried gaze searching my face. "Are you okay?"

I managed a weak nod, murmured something about being fine, and bolted to my room. Once inside, I locked the door and sank to the floor, my chest heaving as tears spilled from my eyes.

I don't want to die.

The thought tore through me like a storm. I didn't want to leave this world, leave *him*. I wanted to live. To grow old with Reyansh. To study hard and make my parents proud, even if they could only watch from heaven. I wanted a future—a future where I could dream of marrying him, of building a life with him, however impossible it seemed.

But Pia's words left no room for hope. Two days. That was all I had to make the most devastating choice of my life. Yet the truth was clear—if Reyansh died, my life would end with his. My soul was bound to his heartbeat.

I buried my face in my hands, sobbing uncontrollably. The pain was too much, the weight unbearable.

A knock at the door startled me. "Sia?" Reyansh's voice was muffled but frantic. "Sia, please open the door."

I didn't answer, my tears flowing harder at the sound of his worry.

"Please, Sia. For God's sake, open the damn door!" His tone cracked, laced with desperation.

After a few moments, I wiped my face hastily and got to my feet, unlocking the door with trembling hands.

Reyansh stood there, his expression a mixture of fear and anguish. The second he saw me, he pulled me into a fierce embrace, holding me so tightly it was as if he feared I would vanish.

"What's wrong, Sia?" he asked, his voice low but insistent as he cupped my face in his hands. "Tell me the truth." His piercing gaze locked onto mine, refusing to let me hide.

I didn't know what came over me. I stepped closer, shutting my eyes as I pressed my tear-stained lips to his. His cold, soft lips froze under mine for a moment, but then he responded, his arms tightening around me.

"This," I whispered, pulling back just enough to meet his eyes, "this is the truth."

Reyansh's eyes were wide, questions swirling within them, but I didn't let him speak.

"I love you, Reyansh," I said, my voice breaking as tears began to fall again. "I need you to know that. I owe my life to you, and I am nothing without you." My words spilled out in a torrent, raw and desperate. "You have to know."

And then the dam broke. I sobbed into his chest, my tears soaking his shirt as he stood frozen in place. Slowly, his arms came around me, holding me as though his touch could shield me from the storm raging within.

He said nothing, but his silence was comforting in its own way. In that moment, words weren't needed. His embrace was enough—a fragile promise to face the impossible together.

XVIII

I pulled on my long black coat, wrapping a red muffler snugly around my neck, and closed the door behind me with a soft, deliberate click. For a moment, I stood motionless, staring at the swirling snow outside. The wind carried a faint howl, its mournful tone filling the silence that stretched around me.

Two days. That was all the time I had left.

The thought weighed heavily on me, gnawing at the edges of my resolve as I stepped out into the frozen world. The streets were blanketed in snow, each step muffling the sound of the outside world and leaving the air still and hauntingly quiet.

I didn't know how it would happen—how my life would end. Would it be quick? A sudden collapse? Or slow and drawn-out, like slipping beneath the ice? My imagination ran wild, but the uncertainty only tightened the knot in my chest. What I did know was that this choice, as unbearable as it was, had to be mine. Pia wasn't going to take that from me.

Last night had been a haze of tension and silence. After my breakdown, neither Reyansh nor I spoke of it. He didn't press, and I was grateful for it. In late afternoon, he'd left for his Grim Reaper duties, leaving me alone to face what lay ahead.

I'd called Pia, arranging to meet at the rain shelter near the cemetery—a place where the veil between life and death felt thin. The roads stretched before me, treacherous under a blanket of fresh snow. Each step was cautious, deliberate, my boots crunching against the ice as I tried to steady myself. The streetlights cast long, distorted shadows that swayed in the wind, making every darkened corner seem alive.

By the time I reached the rain shelter, the snow had paused, leaving the world eerily still. Pia stood there, her silhouette framed against the gray, cloud-heavy sky. She looked almost ethereal, her bright yellow dress untouched by the elements, her hair falling neatly around her shoulders. I wrapped my coat tighter, the sharp cold biting at my skin, but Pia seemed unbothered. Destiny doesn't feel the cold, I thought.

Without turning, she spoke, her voice cutting through the silence as if she had sensed me. "So, why have I been summoned?"

"Summoned?" I repeated, rolling my eyes. "What are you, a Victorian duchess? I called you to give you my answer."

She turned then, a smirk curling on her lips. Her gaze was steady, almost amused. “So much drama for this,” she teased. “Let me guess—you’ve chosen Reyansh.”

Her words sent a jolt through me, but I nodded slowly. “Yes,” I said, my voice quiet but firm. “Save him. You told me it was my fate to die, and I won’t ask you to change that. Let me die. Without Reyansh, I would die anyway.”

For the first time, her smirk faltered. Something flickered in her expression—sympathy, perhaps, or understanding—before her composure returned. “If that’s your wish,” she said evenly, “then it will be fulfilled.”

A bitter laugh escaped me, dry and hollow. “If that’s my wish,” I repeated, my words tasting like ash.

Her gaze softened slightly, the playful facade fading. “You don’t understand the gravity of this,” she said. “This is beyond human comprehension. I don’t expect you to understand, nor do I blame you. I am bound by the laws of existence, Sia. To go against them would unravel everything.”

“I know,” I murmured. “I don’t blame you. I just needed to tell you… and to ask you to protect him.”

With that, I turned and walked away, my boots crunching against the snow as the cold wind whipped against my face.

"Sia."

Her voice stopped me in my tracks, sending a shiver down my spine. I turned, reluctant, to see her stepping closer. Her expression had shifted, her usual aloofness replaced by something softer.

Without warning, she pulled me into a hug, her warmth jarring. Leaning close, she whispered, "You were a wonderful human being."

Her words clung to me like a shadow as I stepped back, nodding stiffly before breaking into a run. My breath formed clouds in the frigid air, my mind racing.

Her voice echoed in my thoughts. *You were a wonderful human being.* The phrasing was wrong—off. It sounded like something you'd say to someone who was already gone.

The streets stretched endlessly before me, each step slower as the snow grew heavier, dulling my senses. The world around me felt unreal, like the moments before waking from a nightmare.

A sharp screech jolted me from my thoughts.

The sound of tires skidding against the icy road pierced the silence, echoing eerily in the stillness of the snowy street. My heart leaped into my throat, my body freezing instinctively as my mind scrambled to process what was happening.

Before I could react, an arm wrapped tightly around my torso, yanking me backward with such force that my boots slipped against the slick ground. Panic surged through me, and I thrashed violently, clawing at the arm that held me in its vice-like grip.

"Let me go!" I screamed, my voice raw with fear.

The man didn't respond. His face was hidden beneath a black mask, leaving only his cold, emotionless eyes visible. He was terrifyingly strong, his grip unyielding as he dragged me toward his dark red car. My mind raced, my breaths coming in short, panicked gasps.

I dug my heels into the ground, twisting and turning with all the strength I could muster, but it was no use. His gloved hand clamped over my mouth as I tried to scream again, muffling the sound.

Then, without warning, his free hand struck me across the face. The sharp sting of the slap radiated through my cheek, and for a moment, the world seemed to tilt. My body faltered, the blow leaving me dazed, and my resistance ceased just long enough for him to tighten his hold.

Before I could recover, he reached into his pocket and pulled out a syringe. The sight of the needle sent a fresh surge of terror through me, but my limbs felt sluggish, my earlier fight draining from me like water slipping through cracks.

"No!" I managed to choke out, thrashing weakly as he grabbed my arm and pinned it down.

I felt the sharp prick of the needle piercing my skin, the cold liquid seeping into my vein. Panic turned to despair as my vision blurred, the edges darkening as whatever was in the syringe took hold.

My movements grew sluggish, my legs buckling beneath me as my body betrayed me. The last thing I saw was the masked man shoving open the car door, his grip never loosening as he hauled me inside.

Darkness closed in, swallowing me whole. My mind raced even as my body went limp, fragments of thoughts slipping away into the void. *Who is he? What does he want? Is this the end?*

XIX

I forced my eyes against the oppressive darkness, the kind that weighed heavy on my chest and made every breath feel like a struggle. The air was thick and stale, laced with a faint metallic tang that turned my stomach. My head felt foggy, as if I had been submerged in a dream that refused to release its hold.

As the haze lifted, I became acutely aware of my body—weak, unsteady, and unresponsive. Panic set in as I tried to move, only to find my arms pinned behind me. A sharp bite of pain registered at my wrists, where coarse ropes dug into my skin. I tugged against them instinctively, but the bonds held firm.

I was sitting on a cold, hard floor, my legs splayed awkwardly in front of me, every joint stiff and unyielding. My limbs felt like they weren't entirely mine, the aftermath of whatever substance had been forced into my veins.

The faintest light seeped through cracks in the wooden walls around me, barely illuminating the small, suffocating space. A shiver coursed through me as questions flooded my thoughts. *Am I dead?* The absurdity of the idea warred with the eerie silence of the room.

The quiet was suddenly broken by the metallic click of a lock turning.

My heart jumped, the sound slicing through the oppressive stillness. The door creaked open, its slow, deliberate motion grating against my already frayed nerves. A figure stepped inside, their silhouette momentarily obscured by the shadows.

I squinted, my breath catching in my throat as he stepped closer. I whimpered instinctively as recognition hit me. The scratch across his face was unmistakable, a jagged scar I'd seen before. It was him—the man I'd encountered at the cemetery months ago during my fight with Reyansh. His presence had unnerved me then, but now, with his wicked grin stretching across his face, I was paralyzed with dread. Fear pooled in my stomach, a cold, heavy dread that rooted me in place.

He crouched down, his movements unhurried, until we were eye to eye. "Finally," he said, his voice low and rasping. It slithered into the air like a venomous hiss. "I've got you. Took me long enough."

His words carried a sickening triumph, as if he had been waiting for this moment for far too long. My chest tightened as he stood again, his eyes gleaming with satisfaction.

He turned toward the wall, his hand reaching for something. With a sharp *click*, the overhead light buzzed to life.

The room was flooded with a harsh, yellow light that buzzed faintly, casting jagged shadows across the wooden walls. Every crack and streak of grime seemed magnified under the sickly glow, amplifying the oppressive atmosphere. My eyes darted around, trying to make sense of my surroundings.

Against the far wall stood a small, rickety table, its surface cluttered with objects that sent a fresh wave of fear through me. Knives of varying sizes were scattered across it, their blades dulled but stained with rust—or was it something else? A few other tools lay beside them, equally sinister in their design.

But what drew my attention most was a small notebook placed carefully at the center of the table, its edges worn and frayed. It seemed out of place among the violent instruments, its presence almost mocking in its simplicity.

On the walls surrounding me, ten dresses hung ominously, their fabrics stained with dried blood. Each one was different—a collection of sizes, colors, and styles—but they all bore the same haunting evidence of violence. The crimson stains had darkened to an almost black hue, their patterns jagged and erratic, as though the dresses had been part of a struggle.

My stomach twisted, bile rising in my throat as the reality of the scene pressed down on me. This wasn't just a room; it was a monument to something horrific.

The man's voice cut through the suffocating silence, drawing my attention back to him. He stood near the door, his grin widening as he followed my gaze to the table. "I see you've noticed my collection," he said, his tone mockingly casual. "And my notes. Don't worry—you'll have your own page soon enough."

The coldness of his words sent a chill racing down my spine, my breath hitching as I struggled to process the full weight of his intentions.

This wasn't a place of refuge or chance. It was a place of purpose—dark, deliberate purpose.

The man turned back to me, his grin widening. "Now," he said, his tone mockingly cheerful, "shall we get started?"

The man picked up a knife from the table, its blade glinting faintly under the dim, yellow light. He held it with unsettling delicacy, running his finger slowly along its edge as though testing its sharpness. My breath hitched, the sight sending a shiver racing down my spine.

Without a word, he reached into his pocket and pulled out my phone—the one I hadn't even realized was missing. He must have taken it while I was unconscious. My stomach twisted as he casually unlocked it using face recognition, tilting the screen toward me. The impersonal efficiency of the act made my skin crawl.

He scrolled through my call list, his expression calm, almost detached, until he landed on Reyansh's name. A wicked smile spread across his face as he tapped it and held the phone to his ear, the sinister intent behind his actions palpable.

The call connected, and the screen lit up with Reyansh's face. My heart ached at the sight of him—his eyes were bloodshot, his face etched with exhaustion and fear. But what devastated me most was the sight of unshed tears glistening in his eyes as he recognized me.

"Let her go," Reyansh said, his voice trembling but firm. "If you harm her—"

The man cut him off with a mocking laugh. "Harm her? Oh, my dear boy, you've got it all wrong. I'm not here to harm her. I'm here to break *you*." He angled the phone toward me, ensuring Reyansh could see every detail of my terrified expression.

"Lay a finger on her, and I swear you'll see what hellfire truly is," Reyansh growled, his voice low and dangerous.

The man's grin widened, his delight evident. "Oh, I *love* challenges, my friend." His voice dripped with mockery as he turned his attention back to me. With chilling precision, he brought the knife to my cheek and pressed it against my skin.

I winced as the cold steel sliced through flesh, leaving a sharp, stinging pain in its wake. Blood trickled down my cheek, warm and thick, as a shallow but deliberate scar took its place—a mark I knew would stay with me forever, were I to live.

"Stop!" Reyansh's voice rang out through the phone, a mixture of fury and desperation.

The man ignored him, tilting the phone back toward his face. "If you want her alive, find me," he barked before ending the call abruptly.

I sat frozen, tears welling in my eyes as he turned back to me, his expression smug. He crouched down to my level, his gloved hand patting my head as though I were some obedient pet. The touch made my stomach churn, and I flinched, wishing I could disappear into the floor.

"Why are you doing this to me?" I asked, my voice barely above a whisper, the words trembling with fear.

He leaned closer, his eyes gleaming with twisted delight. "Because I love challenges. And your precious Reyansh? He gave me the best one yet. Do you remember the night at the cemetery?"

I nodded hesitantly, my mind flashing back to that fateful encounter.

"He's the reason you're here," the man sneered. "He humiliated me. Punched me, dragged you away like I was some sort of villain. I was just trying to *help* you, and yet he treated me like I was nothing. That," he said, his voice dropping to a low growl, "was a mistake."

"It wasn't what you think," I pleaded, desperation lacing my words. "He was just worried about me. He wasn't challenging you."

The man threw his head back and laughed, the sound sharp and cruel. "You really think I care about his intentions? No, sweet girl. All I care about is breaking his ego. And you're my perfect tool for that."

He stood, towering over me as he paced slowly around the room, his boots thudding against the wooden floor. "By the time he gets here, you'll be gone. Dead. And I'll be far away, leaving him with nothing but regret. Oh, and this lovely dress of yours?" He gestured toward me, his grin widening. "It'll make a fine addition to my collection."

My gaze darted to the bloodstained dresses hanging on the walls, my stomach twisting violently at the sight. One dress in particular caught my eye—a tiny, tattered piece, no larger than what a five-year-old would wear.

"You killed them," I said, my voice cracking as the realization hit me. "All of them. Why? They were just children..."

He turned back to me, his head tilting slightly as if considering my question. "Ah, story time, is it?" he said, his tone laced with mockery.

I didn't respond, my eyes locked on the small dress as tears streamed silently down my face.

He chuckled darkly. "You see, I love having control over people, and nothing says control like taking something pure and whole and turning it into something... broken."

His words hung in the air, their weight suffocating. My chest heaved as I struggled to process the sheer cruelty behind them.

"You're a monster," I whispered, my voice trembling with equal parts of fear and anger.

He crouched down again, his face mere inches from mine. "Oh, sweetheart," he said softly, his tone dripping with mock kindness. "You don't know the half of it."

XX

The silence that followed his words was suffocating, broken only by the faint, incessant hum of the overhead light. His face lingered dangerously close to mine, a twisted grin carved into his features, his breath hot and far too close for comfort.

My heart raced, each beat thunderous in my ears as adrenaline coursed through me, stretching every second into an eternity. I averted my gaze, unable to endure the weight of his piercing eyes, but the sight of the bloodstained dresses lining the walls offered no reprieve. Each one seemed to stare back at me, a haunting reminder of the horrors that had unfolded in this room.

He straightened, brushing dust off his pants with an air of unsettling calm, as though his confession was no more significant than idle chatter. "I'll give him credit," he muttered, half to himself, his tone dripping with mock admiration. "Your precious boyfriend really knows how to pick a fight."

I said nothing. My throat was tight, and every shallow breath felt like a struggle. Time had become meaningless—minutes, hours—it all blended into an agonizing blur.

The man turned to the small table, picking up the tattered notebook with an air of casual interest. Flipping through its pages, his expression darkened briefly before a soft chuckle escaped his lips. Without warning, he hurled the notebook at me. It landed with a thud at my feet, splaying open like a dark secret eager to be revealed.

"These," he said, his voice sharp with pride, "are all the girls I've sent to heaven. You'll be number eleven."

Dread gripped me as I stared at the pages, each one adorned with photographs. The man, grinning wickedly, posed with girls—young, terrified, and heartbreakingly beautiful. Their fear was palpable even through the still images, and my stomach churned as I realized the ages of his victims. The youngest couldn't have been more than five, and the oldest, perhaps twenty.

He pointed to a photo of a young woman in her early twenties, her face pale and tight with fear. "You see her? That's Aditi. She was the most challenging one... until now." His voice carried an unnerving mix of pride and nostalgia. "She fought so hard, made me work for it. Took me weeks to lure her to my house." His grin widened, his eyes glinting with a manic light. "And when I finally caught her? Well, I turned her into my favorite meal. A nice meat soup."

My body trembled violently, the realization hitting me like a punch to the gut. He wasn't just a serial killer—he was a monster, a cannibal.

He continued, pacing the room as if reliving his gruesome victories. "But you, Sia... you've outdone her. Catching Aditi only took me a month. You? You've been my most elusive prey. More than three months I've been after you."

My breaths quickened, each one more panicked than the last.

"At first," he said, his voice slipping into a trance-like rhythm, "I thought I'd take you that day on the empty road. But your meddling friend had to show up and ruin my plans. Then, I tried blackmailing your classmate, but that lover of yours..." He spat the words as if they burned his tongue. "He interfered again. So, I went underground, watching, waiting for the perfect moment."

His words droned on, but I wasn't listening anymore. My gaze drifted to the faint rays of sunlight filtering through the cracks in the wooden walls. Morning had arrived, painting the room in a muted glow.

The realization struck like ice in my veins. Morning. This was the day I was going to die.

I glanced back at the notebook lying on the floor, its pages a grim testament to his sick obsession. This wasn't just a crime for him—it was art, a perverse craft, and I was destined to be his next masterpiece.

His voice snapped me back to the present as he chuckled, breaking his monologue. My stomach growled audibly, betraying my hunger. I hadn't eaten since last evening, but the thought of food now seemed like a cruel joke.

"Oh, my poor lamb is hungry," he cooed mockingly. "Let me get you some good fodder." He laughed, striding out of the room and shutting the door behind him.

Tears welled in my eyes as despair clawed at my chest. For one last time, I wanted to see Reyansh. To say goodbye. But fate seemed determined to deny me even that.

The door creaked open again, pulling me from my thoughts. He returned, holding a small package. The greasy smell hit me before I even saw it.

He opened the container, revealing cooked chicken, its oily sheen glistening under the light. My stomach churned.

"Here you go, my lamb," he said with a sinister grin. "I brought this with so much love, just for you."

"I'm vegetarian," I whispered, my voice barely audible.

"Oh, I know." His grin widened. "That's why I brought chicken." He plucked a piece from the container and, despite my feeble struggles, shoved it into my mouth.

I gagged, the oily texture making me retch. Moments later, I vomited, the stench of bile mingling with the chicken as it splattered onto the floor around me. I sat in the mess, my cheeks burning with humiliation and disgust.

He stood back, laughing, my despair only deepening his amusement.

"What are you waiting for?" I snapped, frustration overpowering my fear. "Why don't you just kill me already?"

He tilted his head, his expression thoughtful. "There's a time for everything, my dear. I want to kill you the moment your boyfriend gets close. I want him to live the rest of his miserable life knowing that if he'd been just one minute faster, you could've been saved."

With that, he left again, the door creaking shut behind him.

Minutes stretched into hours. The glow of the sun faded, replaced by the eerie stillness of night. Darkness enveloped the room, and I sat in silence, waiting for the inevitable.

The door opened once more, breaking the quiet. He stepped inside, his expression alight with manic excitement. "He'll be here any minute now," he said gleefully. "I got the news from my sources. It's time for some fun."

He grabbed his camera, holding it up as if this were a joyous occasion. "Let's make some memories, shall we?"

The first click of the camera made me flinch. He took selfie after selfie, his grin stretching wider with each one. Then he pulled me to my feet and dragged me to the wall, his fingers digging painfully into my arm.

"I want you to look as miserable as possible," he sneered.

Before I could brace myself, he drew his knife and slashed me—across my waist, my arms, my legs. The pain was sharp and searing, stealing my breath with each cut. Tears streamed down my face as I whimpered, helpless against his cruelty.

"Let's make this even more interesting," he said, his voice brimming with sadistic glee.

He blindfolded me roughly, plunging me into darkness, and shoved me forward. I stumbled, my feet scraping against the uneven ground. The sharp pricks of shrubs against my legs told me we were outside.

The walk seemed to stretch on forever. My legs grew weaker with every step, the raw, stinging pain of my wounds intensifying as sharp twigs and brambles clawed at my skin. Each breath I took was ragged, like the last whispers of a life slipping away. After what felt like an eternity, we finally came to a halt.

With a rough, sudden motion, he pulled the blindfold away. The moon's pale glow pricked my eyes, and I blinked, adjusting to the dim light. We stood at the forest's edge, where the ground dropped steeply into a shadowy cliffside road that curled around far below.

He faced me, his hands fidgeting with barely contained anticipation. "Any last wishes?" he mocked, his voice laced with feigned sympathy.

I swallowed, the dryness in my throat making my voice brittle. "I want to see Reyansh," I whispered, each word faltering. "Just once more. Please."

He laughed—a sound so hollow, it resonated in the still night. "Oh, sweetheart," he cooed, his voice syrupy and cruel. "You'll see him soon... in heaven."

The knife glinted in his hand as he raised it, poised to strike. I braced myself, eyes shut tight, waiting for the searing pain. But instead, there was a sudden thud and the sharp grunt of impact. I opened my eyes to see Reyansh, a storm of fury and desperation etched on his face, lunging at the man, fists pounding down in a frenzy.

The night exploded into chaos. Shouts and the clash of bodies filled the air as Reyansh fought, a blur of raw, unrelenting strength. His movements were precise, every blow a declaration of his unyielding will. The kidnapper howled, trying to twist away, but Reyansh's rage was an unstoppable force. His fists found their mark again and again, the sound of bone meeting bone, the sickening thud of a punch landing, the cries of pain that shattered the night.

The man staggered, his eyes wide with terror and pain, but Reyansh didn't stop. He continued, striking with the fury of a storm, his blows leaving deep, bruising marks, his breath ragged and wild. He took one step back, his fists raised, eyes locked on the man's face. The kidnapper lunged again, eyes wild, desperation clawing at his features, but Reyansh met him head-on, driving him backward. With one final, shattering blow, the man crumpled, eyes staring up at the dark sky as he fell to the ground, motionless.

Reyansh stood above him, chest heaving, eyes red with fury and exhaustion. He turned, his gaze catching mine, and a fleeting, broken smile crossed his lips. He took a step forward, the weight of every passing second pressing down on us. My heart raced as I reached for him, tears blurring my vision.

But before I could run to him, to feel his arms around me, the kidnapper's body jerked, a wild, unnatural motion. He sprang up with a final, lethal resolve, eyes gleaming with the last remnants of his dark power. A blade flashed in the moonlight, piercing Reyansh's heart. My scream cut through the night as Reyansh crumpled, his hand clutching at his chest, the life fading from his eyes.

He caught the killer's neck in a vice-like grip, eyes meeting mine in a look that spoke of love, sacrifice, and farewell. Both of them fell, tumbling off the edge into the abyss below. I screamed, a raw, aching sound that splintered the night. I lunged forward, but something—someone—pulled me back.

I twisted, frantic, and found Pia's strong arms wrapped around me, holding me back as my heart broke in a thousand different ways.

"No!" I screamed, thrashing against her, the weight of grief and rage burning in my veins. "You're a liar, Pia! You promised me he would live! He's survived so many times before. He's invincible!"

"This was his fate, Sia," Pia said, her voice soft but unyielding. "It had to end this way. His pain had to end. This was the only way to grant him peace."

"No!" I howled, tears streaming down my face, a torrent of despair. "He can't be gone. Not him. Not after everything."

Pia's eyes, full of an ancient sadness, met mine. "His heart had grown weak, Sia. He was already dead—a Grim Reaper, who was never meant to have a beating heart. When he began to care for you, when he attached himself to the warmth of the human world, that heart grew frail. But it wasn't meant to survive. It needed peace too."

And so, as the fire of our story died, it left me alone with the memory of a love that defied everything, even death. A tragic end that whispered of sacrifice and of a heart that refused to stop beating until the very end.

As the night cradled me in its silent embrace, I knew this was not just a goodbye. It was the final echo of a love that could never be forgotten—a love that, in the end, was more beautiful and terrible than anything else in the world.

EPILOGUE

"I loved every bit of it, but the only part I didn't like was when you killed Reyansh." The young reader's eyes, wide and earnest, searched mine for answers as she clutched the book to her chest.

A small, bittersweet smile played on my lips. I had heard this sentiment countless times at book signings, but it never failed to touch me. "But dear, it was his fate. He had to go." I said, signing another copy with a flourish, the pen scratching against the paper as my heart twisted at the memory.

"But he lived for centuries! He could have had a few more years with Sia. They could have grown old together and left in peace," she pressed, her voice wavering with emotion.

"I wish I could have changed that," I said softly, the words carrying more weight than she could know.

"You were their fate," she muttered, half accusing, half resigned. The sentiment stung, but it was true. My words had given life to a story that neither I nor the characters could escape.

Twenty years had passed since that fateful night. I had grown from a young girl into a woman, completing my education and forging a career as a journalist. Reyansh was gone, and so was the man who had tried to end my life. The next morning, the headlines were filled with news of a man's body found on the main road, which police initially suspected was a suicide. It wasn't until later that it was revealed he was a wanted serial killer, a shadow haunting multiple states. But none of that drama ever touched me; I stayed safely outside of its reach, seeking only the truth that mattered.

I had longed to bring Reyansh into the world's light, to reveal him as more than just a myth, a dark figure of stories. I wanted people to know there had been a man named Reyansh who walked among us—a noble soul, a true lover whose heart, though bound by the curse of death, was more alive than any mortal's. That's why I had poured our story into words. Our love, as tragic as it was, had to become eternal.

As I stepped out of the mall where my book signing had taken place, the sky above me darkened, and the first soft droplets of rain began to fall. They kissed my face, cool and comforting, as if Reyansh himself had sent them, whispering his presence through the heavens. Each drop spoke of his eternal touch, weaving into the rain's soft symphony, the wind's gentle sigh, and the silent moments I found solitude in. It was as though he lingered around me, an unseen but undeniable part of my world, reminding me that love, once ignited, never truly fades.

"He's proud of you," a familiar voice said, gentle and knowing. I turned to see her: destiny, the same sixteen-year-old girl who had appeared to me years ago in that dark forest. She hadn't aged a day; she was ageless, eternal, a reminder that even time itself had no hold over certain things.

A tear traced a path down my cheek as I smiled at her, a smile filled with grief, gratitude, and acceptance. Before I could speak, she winked, a playful, wistful expression on her face, and vanished into thin air, leaving only the lingering scent of rain.

I clutched the copy of my novel, *For the Love of Death*, to my chest and took a deep breath. The city lights blurred with raindrops, shimmering like a sea of stars, each one a memory, a moment that I had carried with me. I whispered into the wind in hope that it would take my message to him, "Thank you, Reyansh. For everything."

And with that, I let the rain wash over me, feeling the quiet promise of forever.

The End

Printed by Libri Plureos GmbH in Hamburg, Germany

9 789369 540433